The Rapture: Details of the Second Coming of Christ

Bill Vincent

Published by RWG Publishing, 2021.

While every precaution has been taken in the preparation of this book, the publisher assumes no responsibility for errors or omissions, or for damages resulting from the use of the information contained herein.

THE RAPTURE: DETAILS OF THE SECOND COMING OF CHRIST

First edition. July 29, 2021.

Copyright © 2021 Bill Vincent.

Written by Bill Vincent.

Also by Bill Vincent

Building a Prototype Church: Divine Strategies Released
Experience God's Love: By Revival Waves of Glory School of the Supernatural
Glory: Expanding God's Presence
Glory: Increasing God's Presence
Glory: Kingdom Presence of God
Glory: Pursuing God's Presence
Glory: Revival Presence of God
Rapture Revelations: Jesus Is Coming
The Prototype Church: Heaven's Strategies for Today's Church
The Secret Place of God's Power
Transitioning Into a Prototype Church: New Church Arising
Spiritual Warfare Made Simple
Aligning With God's Promises
A Closer Relationship With God
Armed for Battle: Spiritual Warfare Battle Commands
Breakthrough of Spiritual Strongholds
Desperate for God's Presence: Understanding Supernatural Atmospheres
Destroying the Jezebel Spirit: How to Overcome the Spirit Before It Destroys You!
Discerning Your Call of God

Glory: Expanding God's Presence: Discover How to Manifest God's Glory

Glory: Kingdom Presence Of God: Secrets to Becoming Ambassadors of Christ

Satan's Open Doors: Access Denied

Spiritual Warfare: The Complete Collection

The War for Spiritual Battles: Identify Satan's Strategies

Understanding Heaven's Court System: Explosive Life Changing Secrets

A Godly Shaking: Don't Create Waves

Faith: A Connection of God's Power

Global Warning: Prophetic Details Revealed

Overcoming Obstacles

Spiritual Leadership: Kingdom Foundation Principles

Glory: Revival Presence of God: Discover How to Release Revival Glory

Increasing Your Prophetic Gift: Developing a Pure Prophetic Flow

Millions of Churches: Why Is the World Going to Hell?

The Supernatural Realm: Discover Heaven's Secrets

The Unsearchable Riches of Christ: Chosen to be Sons of God

Deep Hunger: God Will Change Your Appetite Toward Him

Defeating the Demonic Realm

Glory: Increasing God's Presence: Discover New Waves of God's Glory

Growing In the Prophetic: Developing a Prophetic Voice

Healing After Divorce: Grace, Mercy and Remarriage

Love is Waiting

Awakening of Miracles: Personal Testimonies of God's Healing Power

Deception and Consequences Revealed: You Shall Know the Truth and the Truth Shall Set You Free
Overcoming the Power of Lust
Are You a Follower of Christ: Discover True Salvation
Cover Up and Save Yourself: Revealing Sexy is Not Sexy
Heaven's Court System: Bringing Justice for All
The Angry Fighter's Story: Harness the Fire Within
The Wrestler: The Pursuit of a Dream
Beginning the Courts of Heaven: Understanding the Basics
Breaking Curses: Legal Rights in the Courts of Heaven
Writing and Publishing a Book: Secrets of a Christian Author
How to Write a Book: Step by Step Guide
The Anointing: Fresh Oil of God's Presence
Spiritual Leadership: Kingdom Foundation Principles Second Edition
The Courts of Heaven: How to Present Your Case
The Jezebel Spirit: Tactics of Jezebel's Control
Heaven's Angels: The Nature and Ranking of Angels
Don't Know What to Do?: Discover Promotion in the Wilderness
Word of the Lord: Prophetic Word for 2020
The Coronavirus Prophecy
Increase Your Anointing: Discover the Supernatural
Apostolic Breakthrough: Birthing God's Purposes
The Healing Power of God: Releasing the Power of the Holy Spirit
The Secret Place of God's Power: Revelations of God's Word
The Rapture: Details of the Second Coming of Christ
Increase of Revelation and Restoration: Reveal, Recover & Restore

Restoration of the Soul: The Presence of God Changes Everything

Building a Prototype Church: The Church is in a Season of Profound of Change

Keys to Receiving Your Miracle: Miracles Happen Today

The Resurrection Power of God: Great Exploits of God

Transitioning to the Prototype Church: The Church is in a Season of Profound of Transition

Waves of Revival: Expect the Unexpected

The Stronghold of Jezebel: A True Story of a Man's Journey

Glory: Pursuing God's Presence: Revealing Secrets

Like a Mighty Rushing Wind

Steps to Revival

Supernatural Power

The Goodness of God

The Secret to Spiritual Strength

The Glorious Church's Birth: Understanding God's Plan For Our Lives

God's Presence Has a Profound Impact On Us

Spiritual Battles of the Mind: When All Hell Breaks Loose, Heaven Sends Help

A Godly Shaking Coming to the Church: Churches are Being Rerouted

Relationship with God in a New Way

The Spirit of God's Anointing: Using the Holy Spirit's Power in You

The Magnificent Church: God's Power Is Being Manifested

Miracles Are Awakened: Today is a Day of Miracles

Prepared to Fight: The Battle of Deliverance

The Journey of a Faithful: Adhering to the teachings of Jesus Christ

Ascension to the Top of Spiritual Mountains: Putting an End to Pain Cycles

After Divorce Recovery: When I Think of Grace, I Think of Mercy and Remarriage

A Greater Sense of God's Presence: Learn How to Make God's Glory Visible

Do Not Allow the Enemy to Steal: To a Crown of Righteousness, a Crown of Thorns

There Are Countless Churches: What is the Cause of Global Doom?

Creating a Model Church: The Church is Undergoing Considerable Upheaval

Developing Your Prophetic Ability: Creating a Flow of Pure Prophetic Intent

Christ's Limitless Riches Are Unsearchable: God Has Chosen Us to Be His Sons

Faith is a Link Between God's Might and Ours

Increasing the Presence of God: The Revival of the End-Times Is Approaching

Getting a Prophecy for Yourself: Unlocking Your Prophecies with Prophetic Keys

Getting Rid of the Jezebel Spirit: Before the Spirit Destroys You, Here's How to Overcome It!

Getting to Know Heaven's Court System: Secrets That Will Change Your Life

God's Resurrected Presence: Revival Glory is Being Released

God's Presence In His Kingdom: Secrets to Becoming Christ's Ambassadors

God's Healing Ability: The Holy Spirit's Power is Being Released

God's Power of Resurrection: God's Great Exploits

- Heaven's Supreme Court: Providing Equal Justice for All
- Increasing God's Presence in Our Lives: God's Glory Has Reached New Heights
- Jezebel's Stronghold: This is the Story of an Actual Man's Journey
- Making the Shift to the Model Church: The Church Is In the Midst of a Major Shift
- Overcoming Lust's Influence: The Way to Victory
- Pursuing God's Presence: Disclosing Information
- The Plan to Take Over America: Restoring, We the People and the Power of God
- Revelation and Restoration Are Increasing: The Process That Reveals, Recovers, and Restores
- Burn In the Presence of the Lord
- Revival Tidal Waves: Be Prepared for the Unexpected
- Taking down the Demonic Realm: Curses and Revelations of Demonic Spirits
- The Apocalypse: Details about Christ's Second Coming
- The Hidden Resource of God's Power
- The Open Doors of Satan: Access is Restricted
- The Secrets to Getting Your Miracle
- The Truth About Deception and Its Consequences
- The Universal World: Discover the Mysteries of Heaven
- Warning to the World: Details of Prophecies Have Been Revealed
- Wonders and Significance: God's Glory in New Waves
- Word of the Lord
- Why Is There No Lasting Revival: It's Time For the Next Move of God
- A Double New Beginning: A Prophetic Word, the Best Is Yet to Come

Your Most Productive Season Ever: The Anointing to Get Things Done
Break Free From Prison: No More Bondage for the Saints
Breaking Strongholds: Taking Steps to Freedom
Carrying the Glory of God: Igniting the End Time Revival
Breakthrough Over the Enemies Attack on Resources: An Angel Called Breakthrough
Days of Breakthrough: Your Time is Now
Empowered For the Unprecedented: Extraordinary Days Ahead
The Ultimate Guide to Self-Publishing: How to Write, Publish, and Promote Your Book for Free
The Art of Writing: A Comprehensive Guide to Crafting Your Masterpiece
The Non-Fiction Writer's Guide: Mastering Engaging Narratives
Spiritual Leadership (Large Print Edition): Kingdom Foundation Principles
Desperate for God's Presence (Large Print Edition): Understanding Supernatural Atmospheres
From Writer to Marketer: How to Successfully Promote Your Self-Published Book
Unleashing Your Inner Author: A Step-by-Step Guide to Crafting Your Own Bestseller
Becoming a YouTube Sensation: A Guide to Success
The Art of Content Creation: Tips and Tricks for YouTube
Signs and Wonders Revelations: Experience Heaven on Earth

Watch for more at
https://revivalwavesofgloryministries.com/.

Introduction

Much has been written and taught about the coming of Christ for His Church. Unfortunately, most of our modern day teachings on this most important doctrine are misleading to say the very least. A careful scrutiny of the Scriptures will reveal the truth about the second coming of Christ, which we generally refer to as "the rapture".

In this book I have set out to correct the most obvious errors of the pre-tribulation doctrine and to establish the basic foundation for understanding the truth of the matter. Great care is taken to follow the guidelines of Scripture and the Biblical basis of doctrinal interpretation, precept upon precept and line upon line. This is the only method of interpretation used in the pages of this book. Since God Himself revealed His method of understanding doctrine, it is believed by the author to be the best method to use. Therefore, with Bible in hand, follow along with the Scriptures quoted in this book and see if you don't find truth within its pages.

If you are a lover of truth, I believe you will enjoy this very basic presentation of Biblical facts concerning the doctrine of the "gathering together" of Christ's saints unto Himself.

The Resurrection of the Dead

In order to understand the doctrine of the rapture, it is necessary to understand other doctrines of the Scriptures as well. We cannot comprehend any single doctrine without it being precept upon precept, line upon line, here a little, there a little.

Isaiah 28:9, 10 Whom shall he teach knowledge? and whom shall he make to understand doctrine? them that are weaned from the milk, and drawn from the breasts. For precept must be upon precept, precept upon precept; line upon line, line upon line; here a little, and there a little.

In studying the rapture, we must look at the entire Bible in order to come to a reasonable conclusion of the matter, rather than picking out isolated verses that seem to justify our particular view of this doctrine. In order to teach the doctrine of the rapture according to the integrity of the Word, we must be able to prove the doctrine with all the available verses of Scripture, not just a few. One of the biblical doctrines that we must know in order to understand the rapture is the doctrine of the resurrection of the dead. Why is the resurrection of the dead so important to comprehending the rapture and the events that must take place prior to it? Simply because the Bible states that the dead in Christ will precede those of us who are alive and remain.

1 Thessalonians 4:16, 17 For the Lord himself shall descend from heaven with a shout, with the voice of the archangel, and with the trump of God: and the dead in Christ shall rise first: Then we which are alive and remain shall be

caught up together with them in the clouds, to meet the Lord in the air: and so shall we ever be with the Lord.

If the dead in Christ must rise first before the believers who are alive at His coming are changed, then it should be of great interest to us to search out the doctrine of the resurrection of the dead.

For example, how many resurrections of the dead are recorded in the Bible? By resurrection of the dead I mean the mass resurrections of the dead, one of which will immediately precede the rapture, not individual resurrections or translations such as Lazarus, Enoch, or Elijah.

It is commonly taught in some circles that there are as many as nine resurrections of the dead. This is an elaborate scheme to defame the Holy Scriptures in an attempt to justify false teaching concerning the rapture. The dead in Christ who will be raised at the rapture are referred to in the Scriptures as the resurrection of the just.

The resurrection of the just is indeed that resurrection of the dead in Christ that occurs immediately before the rapture.

There is much confusion in the Church today as to when Jesus is coming back for His bride. The three most common doctrines that are being taught are the pre-tribulation rapture, Jesus coming before the Great Tribulation, which according to this line of thought is a period of seven years, the mid-tribulation rapture, occurring in the middle of the seven year period known as the seventieth week of Daniel and the post-tribulation rapture which occurs after the entire seven year period has elapsed. One of the greatest stumbling blocks concerning the doctrine of the rapture is a lack of understanding of the doctrine of the resurrection of the dead.

THE RAPTURE: DETAILS OF THE SECOND COMING OF CHRIST

If we can know for certain when the resurrection of the just, also known as the first resurrection occurs, then we can know with greater certainty when the rapture occurs in relation to the seven year period of time known as The Seventieth Week of Daniel. Let's take a look at the resurrection of the dead according to the Bible.

John 5:28, 29 Marvel not at this: for the hour is coming, in the which all that are in the graves shall hear his voice, And shall come forth; they that have done good, unto the resurrection of life; and they that have done evil, unto the resurrection of damnation.

Acts 24:14, 15 But this I confess unto thee, that after the way which they call heresy, so worship I the God of my fathers, believing all things which are written in the law and in the prophets: And have hope toward God, which they themselves also allow, that there shall be a resurrection of the dead, both of the just and unjust.

Luke 14:14 And thou shalt be blessed; for they cannot recompense thee: for thou shalt be recompensed at the resurrection of the just.

In searching the Scriptures we can find only two mass resurrections of the dead. They are referred to as the resurrection of the just and the resurrection of the unjust. They are also referred to as the first and second, or final resurrection.

Revelations 20:4-6 And I saw thrones, and they sat upon them, and judgment was given unto them: and I saw the souls of them that were beheaded for the witness of Jesus, and for the word of God, and which had not worshipped the beast, neither his image, neither had received his mark upon their foreheads, or in their hands; and they lived and reigned with Christ a thousand years. But the rest of the dead lived not again until the thousand years were finished. This is the first resurrection. Blessed and holy is he that hath part in the first resurrection: on such the second death hath no power, but they shall be priests of God and of Christ, and shall reign with him a thousand years.

In investigating these verses of Scripture, understanding that according to the Bible there are but two mass resurrections of the dead, we can easily conclude that the rapture takes place AFTER the great tribulation, considering the fact that those who took part in the first resurrection were in the earth during the time of the rule of anti-Christ, proven by the fact that they did not receive his mark, nor did they worship him. Just how many were there that came out of this great tribulation?

Revelations 7:9-14 After this I beheld, and, lo, a great multitude, which no man could number, of all nations, and kindreds, and people, and tongues, stood before the throne, and before the Lamb, clothed with white robes, and palms in their hands; And cried with a loud voice, saying, Salvation to our God which sitteth upon the throne, and unto the Lamb. And all the angels stood round about the throne, and about the elders and the four beasts, and fell before the throne on their faces, and worshipped God, Saying, Amen: Blessing, and glory, and wisdom, and thanksgiving, and honour, and power, and might, be unto our God for ever and ever. Amen. And one of the elders answered, saying unto me, What are these which are arrayed in white robes? and whence came they? And I said unto him, Sir, thou knowest. And he said to me, These are they which came out of great tribulation, and have washed their robes, and made them white in the blood of the Lamb.

THE RAPTURE: DETAILS OF THE SECOND COMING OF CHRIST

In studying the rapture, we would do well to search out what Jesus taught on the subject and then see how all other Scriptures line up with His teachings. If we can believe anyone's teaching on the rapture, surely we can believe what Jesus taught. His teaching on the timing of the rapture is so clear that we so easily stumble over it.

He said;

Matthew 24:29-31 Immediately after the tribulation of those days shall the sun be darkened, and the moon shall not give her light, and the stars shall fall from heaven, and the powers of the heavens shall be shaken: And then shall appear the sign of the Son of man in heaven: and then shall all the tribes of the earth mourn, and they shall see the Son of man coming in the clouds of heaven with power and great glory. And he shall send his angels with a great sound of a trumpet, and they shall gather together his elect from the four winds, from one end of heaven to the other.

Some might say that those who came out of the great tribulation are those who were saved after the Church was raptured. It is generally taught that after the Church is raptured, those who were unbelieving and skeptical toward the gospel, will at this time realize their error and turn to Jesus Christ and be saved.

Most ministers teach that the loved ones and families of those who do not make it in the rapture will have another chance to accept Jesus and be saved. Can this be true? Will those who do not go in the rapture have another opportunity to be saved? Again, let's go to the Bible.

Luke 17:26-30 And as it was in the days of Noe, so shall it be also in the days of the Son of man. They did eat, they drank, they married wives, they were given in marriage, until the day that Noe entered into the ark, and the flood came, and destroyed them all. Likewise also as it was in the days of Lot; they did eat, they drank, they bought, they sold, they planted, they builded; But the same day that Lot went out of Sodom it rained fire and brimstone from heaven, and destroyed them all. Even thus shall it be in the day when the Son of man is revealed.

Matthew 25:1-12 Then shall the kingdom of heaven be likened unto ten virgins, which took their lamps, and went forth to meet the bridegroom. And five of them were wise, and five were foolish. They that were foolish took their lamps, and took no oil with them: But the wise took oil in their vessels with their lamps. While the bridegroom tarried, they all slumbered and slept. And at midnight there was a cry made, Behold, the bridegroom cometh; go ye out to meet him. Then all those virgins arose, and trimmed their lamps. And the foolish said unto the wise, Give us of your oil; for our lamps are gone out. But the wise answered, saying, Not so; lest there be not enough for us and you: but go ye rather to them that sell, and buy for yourselves. And while they went to buy, the bridegroom came; and they that were ready went in with him to the marriage: and the door was shut. Afterward came also the other virgins, saying, Lord, Lord, open to us. But he answered and said, Verily I say unto you, I know you not.

In the above verses of Scripture, it is quite clear that those who do not go in the rapture will remain on the earth to suffer the wrath of God which will begin on the same day that the Church is raptured. There is a great deal of confusion as to what the wrath of God is and when it will be poured out upon the earth. The wrath of God does not last for seven years as is commonly taught and neither is the rule of the anti - Christ considered to be the wrath of God. We will see later that the "Great Tribulation" is the devil's wrath against all mankind and has absolutely nothing to do with the wrath of God.

Since the coming of the Lord and the gathering together of the saints will be just like it was in the days of Noah and Lot, there are some questions that must be answered.

Was it possible for anyone to be saved after the door was shut on the ark and the rain began? NO! Was it possible for anyone to be saved after Lot and his family came out of Sodom? NO!

Jesus said it will be the same way when He comes and the Church is gathered together. No one will have the opportunity to be saved after the rapture. Those who are left behind will face a more terrible fate than the great tribulation. They will face the unbridled wrath of God with no hope of being saved. We will also see according to the Bible that the seven year period of time known as Daniel's seventieth week is not the great tribulation as many suppose. According to the Scriptures, the great tribulation does not begin until the middle of the week, or three and one-half years after the seven year period begins.

This particular doctrinal error, along with many others, has caused the Church to believe a lie, that is; the doctrine of the pre-tribulation rapture. You may think that is strong language to say that the pre-tribulation rapture teaching is a lie and I would agree with you. But straight truth is desperately needed today in a society and a Church where immorality and self-serving doctrine is the fare of the day. There were some in Paul's day who taught false doctrine concerning end-time events. They were teaching that the resurrection of the dead had already taken place. What did Paul have to say about this doctrinal error? Did he just ignore it and hope it would straighten itself out? Look at how Paul dealt with this doctrinal error and how he viewed those who were teaching false doctrine.

2 Timothy 2:15-18 Study to shew thyself approved unto God, a workman that needeth not to be ashamed, rightly dividing the word of truth. But shun profane and vain babblings: for they will increase unto more ungodliness. And their word will eat as doth a canker: of whom is Hymenaeus and Philetus; Who concerning the truth have erred, saying that the resurrection is past already; and overthrow the faith of some.

The pre-tribulation rapture doctrine is doing the same as the false doctrine propagated by Hymenaeus and Philetus. It is overthrowing the faith of some who hear and prescribe to it. This doctrine that teaches salvation after the rapture of the Church has the potential to lead many into the bowels of hell and to spend eternity in the lake of fire that burns with fire and brimstone. Now is the time to preach the gospel to your family and friends so they can be saved! Don't trust in a lie that can rob them of eternal life! When Jeremiah prophesied to the nation of Israel that they would go into captivity for a period of seventy years, according to the word of the Lord, no one wanted to believe him. The same is true today of those who are teaching that the Church will have to endure the great tribulation, or in effect, go into captivity. These teachers of truth are received about as well today as Jeremiah was in his day.

Of course there were the false prophets who contradicted the word of the Lord through Jeremiah the truth and prophesied to and taught the people what they wanted to hear. The same is true today. False doctrine is clouding the truth and many false prophets and false teachers are prophesying to and teaching the people what they want to hear. What will be the consequences for those who prophesy and teach lies? Hear what God said to Hananiah, a prophet who prophesied lies to the people of God concerning the seventy years of captivity that Jeremiah prophesied of in the word of the Lord:

Jeremiah 28:10-17 Then Hananiah the prophet took the yoke from off the prophet Jeremiah's neck, and brake it. And Hananiah spake in the presence of all the people, saying, Thus saith the LORD; Even so will I break the yoke of Nebuchadnezzar king of Babylon from the neck of all nations within the space of two full years. And the prophet Jeremiah went his way. Then the word of the LORD came unto Jeremiah the prophet, after that Hananiah the prophet had broken the yoke from off the neck of the prophet Jeremiah, saying, Go and tell Hananiah, saying, Thus saith the LORD; Thou hast broken the yokes of wood; but thou shalt make for them yokes of iron. For thus saith the LORD of hosts, the God of Israel; I have put a yoke of iron upon the neck of all these nations, that they may serve Nebuchadnezzar king of Babylon; and they shall serve him: and I have given him the beasts of the field also. Then said the prophet Jeremiah unto Hananiah the prophet, Hear now, Hananiah; The LORD hath not sent thee; but thou makest this people to trust in a lie. Therefore thus saith the LORD; Behold, I will cast thee from off the face of the earth: this year thou shalt die, because thou hast taught rebellion against the

LORD. So Hananiah the prophet died the same year in the seventh month.

Of course, we don't see many prophets and teachers' dying today because of teaching false doctrine and prophesying lies. For this reason and because of the fact that most teachers are teaching it, it seems that God must approve of the pre-tribulation doctrine.

Consequently, there is not a great regard for purity of doctrine in the Church and there is very little fear of God in teaching doctrine. Many believe that we can teach whatever we believe personally and what we receive by "revelation" from the Holy Spirit. The problem with that is that obviously we are not all hearing from the same spirit. Some of us are hearing from a spirit of error and believing that we are hearing from God. Nearly everyone who teaches the rapture doctrine claims to have received his revelation from the Holy Spirit. I would like to make it clear, based on the authority of the Holy Scriptures, which the doctrine of the Church being raptured before the great tribulation begins, pre-tribulation rapturism is a false doctrine. I do not mean to say that all who teach it are false teachers, but do not be deceived, it is a false doctrine! I am not opposed to my brethren in Christ who teach the pre-tribulation doctrine, but I am very much opposed to the doctrine itself. Most ministers who teach the pre-tribulation doctrine sincerely believe their doctrine is correct and do not intend to lead believers away from the truth of God's Word. But, we are living, I believe, in the very last of the last days and the doctrine of the second coming of Christ and the gathering together of His saints, must be preached and taught accurately. And it must be taught, "precept upon precept and line upon line". May God give us the grace to come to a unified understanding of this most important doctrine? Many ministers believe that the doctrine is not that important and to avoid controversy, will not teach it. But beloved, please know that this doctrine is extremely important. If you believe that your family and friends will have another opportunity to be saved after the gathering together, you may be slack in preaching the gospel to them. Please remember, today is the day of salvation. Preach the gospel to them and pray for their salvation while the opportunity is still there.

2 Thessalonians 2:3, 4 Let no man deceive you by any means: for that day shall not come, except there come a falling away first, and that man of sin be revealed, the son of perdition; Who opposeth and exalteth himself above all that is called God, or that is worshipped; so that he as God sitteth in the temple of God, shewing himself that he is God.

Since the rapture cannot occur until the anti-Christ is revealed, which occurs in the middle of the week, the rapture cannot possibly take place until at least three-and-one-half years after the beginning of the seventieth week of Daniel. DO NOT BE DECEIVED!

Some, perhaps most who believe in and teach the pre-tribulation rapture, have been taught this doctrine from others and have been blinded by their traditional understanding. I would challenge anyone who believes in a pre-tribulation rapture to search the Scriptures (all the Scriptures) pertaining to the rapture and events that will occur during the last days and see if all of the Scriptures say the same thing, using of course, the "precept upon precept, line upon line" method of interpreting Scripture. In light of the whole word of God, the doctrine of the pre-tribulation rapture is exposed for what it is, a false doctrine that has slipped into the Church under the appearance of Holy Spirit "revelation."

While the Bible promises persecution and tribulation to the believer just prior to the coming of Christ, this false doctrine promises freedom from persecution and promotes superiority within the body of Christ. Not to mention the fact that, people who will not endure sound doctrine, will pay generously to have their itching ears scratched.

2 Timothy 4:2-4 Preach the word; be instant in season, out of season; reprove, rebuke, exhort with all longsuffering and doctrine. For the time will come when they will not endure sound doctrine; but after their own lusts shall they heap to themselves teachers, having itching ears; And they shall turn away their ears from the truth, and shall be turned unto fables.

I do not mean to imply that all who teach the pre-tribulation doctrine do so for financial gain, but we must look at the millions, perhaps billions of dollars that are being made by teaching this false doctrine. In book stores everywhere, including department stores, these books are offered and sold in abundance. I personally have some very good friends who believe in and teach the pre-tribulation doctrine. We continue to fellowship in the love of Christ, even though we differ on this doctrinal issue. The Scriptures teach us to "endeavor to keep the unity of the Spirit in the bond of peace." This is my position toward those who teach the pre-tribulation error. I love my brethren in Christ and I will not attack them personally, but I will do all that I can to disprove this incorrect doctrine and sound a warning to the Church concerning this damnable doctrine.

Others, who approach doctrine from an intellectual standpoint, miss the revelation from the Holy Spirit on the doctrine of the rapture. These are those who, by carnal reasoning remove the power of God from the Scriptures. They usually do not believe in the power of the Holy Spirit being ministered through His saints through the gifts of the Spirit. Many of them believe in the end doctrine, the belief that the gifts of the Spirit have ceased with the canonization of the Scriptures. They therefore cannot easily receive revelation from the Holy Spirit and consequently their doctrine is based on their natural reasoning, rather than by revelation from the Spirit of truth. Rather than believing the Holy Spirit to reveal truth concerning the Word, they are hard at work to disprove the power of the Scriptures. They do not understand that the Holy Spirit reveals the truth and the power of the word, rather than to disprove it. They do error, not knowing the Scriptures, nor the power of God. Understanding then, according to the Scriptures, that there is no second chance to be saved after the rapture, it is urgent that we preach the gospel to our friends, loved ones and to others while there is still hope.

How tragic it would be if Christians sit back comfortably waiting for the rapture, believing that their families and friends will be saved afterward and then come face-to-face with the reality that they will forever be doomed to eternal torment in the lake of fire that burns with fire and brimstone. This fact in itself should encourage us to study end-time events with an open heart and mind, understanding the word of God and bringing salvation and warning to the unlearned and unbelieving. Many will say that the doctrine of the rapture and end-time events is not that important and that we should avoid it because it is so controversial.

Please consider this; if we were to ignore Bible doctrine simply because it is controversial we would have to ignore all Bible doctrine. How can we disregard something that is given so much place in Scripture and how can we say that it doesn't apply to us and we don't need to know? Martin Luther and many others risked their lives to restore truth to the Church.

Martin Luther's doctrines were certainly controversial and he was himself branded a heretic for daring to oppose the false doctrine of his day. We would still be in the dark ages if not for men like Martin Luther and others who endured ridicule and persecution to bring truth to God's people. Accordingly, some today are daring to go against the religious grain and refute the false doctrine of the pre-tribulation rapture. Some of them are also being branded as heretics by those who oppose the truth. But, thanks be to God, all Christians who love the truth of the Holy Scriptures, are receiving the truth and are sharing that truth with their friends and loved ones. Also, if we believe that we are living in the last days, we should want to understand the events that are just ahead of us, unless we have assumed an ostrich mentality and buried our heads in the sand. To disagree with the pre-tribulation rapture theory is equivalent to denying the faith in the minds of some. This false doctrine has so permeated the thinking of most Christians today that it is almost thought of as blasphemy to disagree with it.

Most of the arguments in favor of pre-tribulation are based on a few Scripture verses, (simply because there are only a few that seem to validate this thought) and fierce argument ranging from character assassination toward those who dare to be of a different opinion and volumes of current events which all somehow seem to prove the pre-tribulation belief and many words of contention which are against of scriptural reference.

The Seventieth Week of Daniel

The seven year period of time known as Daniel's Seventieth Week will begin with the confirming of a covenant for a period of seven years. The one who confirms the covenant is assumed to be the anti-Christ and the many that the covenant is confirmed with is presumed to be many in Israel, and/or perhaps many nations. The Bible records it this way:

Daniel 9:27 And he shall confirm the covenant with many for one week: and in the midst of the week he shall cause the sacrifice and the oblation to cease, and for the overspreading of abominations he shall make it desolate, even until the consummation, and that determined shall be poured upon the desolate.

This seven year period starts the beginning of the end of time as we know it as a flesh and blood people. After that interval of time is finished, all the dead in Christ who were resurrected at the rapture and the saints who were changed at His coming, will now have a glorified body and time will no longer be of any consequence to us, with the exception of the one-thousand year reign of Christ on the earth. It is during this seven year period that those remaining prophecies that are to be fulfilled before Jesus comes will transpire.

Acts 3:20, 21 And he shall send Jesus Christ, which before was preached unto you: Whom the heaven must receive until the times of restitution of all things, which God hath spoken by the mouth of all his holy prophets since the world began.

This phrase; "until the times of restitution of all things," clearly implies that Jesus cannot come at any moment (the doctrine of imminence), as is commonly taught in regards to the pre-tribulation rapture. As we look closer at the word of God we will find that there are numerous errors associated with the pre-tribulation view. In no way are we opposed to our brethren who teach this doctrinal error, but we are opposed to the error itself. Our hope is that we may all come into an accurate understanding of the rapture and associated events and will end the confusion and division that has been caused by this incorrect doctrine. We also realize that we do not have all the understanding of this doctrine and that we are in need of our brethren with opposing views in order to receive an adequate understanding of the rapture. I am not saying that we can embrace error, but I do believe that we all have some of the truth and as we come together with our portion of the truth we trust that we can arrive at the whole truth by reasoning together in the Scriptures and seeking revelation from the Holy Spirit.

There are many who believe that we will never be able to come into oneness of understanding of the Scriptures, but the Bible teaches that we should.

1 Corinthians 1:10 Now I beseech you, brethren, by the name of our Lord Jesus Christ, that ye all speak the same thing, and that there be no divisions among you; but that ye be perfectly joined together in the same mind and in the same judgment.

In fact, it has been the disagreement of doctrine that has separated the Church and it will be the unity of the Spirit and doctrine that will help unite us again. There is so much to be done to bring the Church together and to the carnal mind it seems impossible to do. But, we must remember that it is God Himself that will bring all things together before He comes for His bride. To think that we can accomplish this feat ourselves is to ascend to the highest heights of pride and arrogance. Actually, just the opposite is true. In the days ahead, it will require a great deal of humility just to follow what God is doing.

The proud will be swept away in their transgression and impudence, believing every lie and deception of the devil that is reserved for these last days, while the humble will shine as great lights in the midst of gross darkness. The Seventieth week of Daniel is divided into two three- and one-half year periods. In the first half we see the beginning of sorrows as described by Jesus in the discourse in,

Matthew 24:4-13 And Jesus answered and said unto them, Take heed that no man deceive you. For many shall come in my name, saying, I am Christ; and shall deceive many. And ye shall hear of wars and rumours of wars: see that ye be not troubled: for all these things must come to pass, but the end is not yet. For nation shall rise against nation, and kingdom against kingdom: and there shall be famines, and pestilences, and earthquakes, in divers places. All these are the beginning of sorrows. Then shall they deliver you up to be afflicted, and shall kill you: and ye shall be hated of all nations for my name's sake. And then shall many be offended, and shall betray one another, and shall hate one another. And many false prophets shall rise, and shall deceive many. And because iniquity shall abound, the love of many shall wax cold. But he that shall endure unto the end, the same shall be saved. Jesus spoke of the great tribulation beginning in the middle of the week, (three and one-half years after the week begins, not at the beginning as is taught in the pre-tribulation doctrine).

Matthew 24:15-21 When ye therefore shall see the abomination of desolation, spoken of by Daniel the prophet, stand in the holy place, (whoso readeth, let him understand:) Then let them which be in Judaea flee into the mountains: Let him which is on the housetop not come down to take any thing out of his house: Neither let him which is in the field return back to take his clothes. And woe unto them that are with child, and to them that give suck in those days! But pray ye that your flight be not in the winter, neither on the sabbath day: For then shall be great tribulation, such as was not since the beginning of the world to this time, no, nor ever shall be.

It will be this second half of Daniel's Seventieth week, the great tribulation, that the Church and Israel will suffer the greatest persecution and trouble of all time.

Matthew 24:21 For then shall be great tribulation, such as was not since the beginning of the world to this time, no, nor ever shall be.

Considering the fact that the Jewish people have suffered horribly at the hands of their enemies ever since their first rebellion as a nation brought on the curses associated with disobedience, it is hard to imagine anything worse than the holocaust at the hands of Hitler and Germany, or some of the times of trouble that are recorded in the Bible. But Jesus said that the great tribulation would be far greater than anything they had ever experienced until that time. Not only will the Jews suffer, but the whole world will be under the rule of anti-Christ

and will be expected to worship him.

Revelations 13:16-18 And he causeth all, both small and great, rich and poor, free and bond, to receive a mark in their right hand, or in their foreheads: And that no man might buy or sell, save he that had the mark, or the name of the beast, or the number of his name. Here is wisdom. Let him that hath understanding count the number of the beast: for it is the number of a man; and his number is Six hundred threescore and six.

Some will say then, how could God allow His own saints to endure this kind of terrible oppression? Aren't we exempt from persecution just as the teachers of the pre-tribulation doctrine have taught us? Isn't this the generation of Christians that will do great exploits for their God and work miracles, signs and wonders? Indeed this is the generation that will do many great works in the name of the Lord; but it is also the generation that will be allowed to suffer the greatest for their Lord.

Daniel 11:32 And such as do wickedly against the covenant shall he corrupt by flatteries: but the people that do know their God shall be strong, and do exploits.

The great tribulation will be such a time of trouble that many will perhaps choose to pledge their allegiance to the anti-Christ rather than suffer for the Lord. Can this really happen? Can Christians actually fall away during this time of testing? One of the signs that will come before the rapture is the great falling away that was spoken of by Paul and Timothy:

2 Thessalonians 2:1-3 Now we beseech you, brethren, by the coming of our Lord Jesus Christ, and by our gathering together unto him, That ye be not soon shaken in mind, or be troubled, neither by spirit, nor by word, nor by letter as from us, as that the day of Christ is at hand. Let no man deceive you

by any means: for that day shall not come, except there come a falling away first, and that man of sin be revealed, the son of perdition;

1 Timothy 4:1 Now the Spirit speaketh expressly, that in the latter times some shall depart from the faith, giving heed to seducing spirits, and doctrines of devils;

Will it really be possible for Christians to fall away and depart from the faith in the time of the Great Tribulation? The Scriptures certainly confirm that fact! Consider this; if many Christians are expecting to be raptured before the Great Tribulation and then find themselves in the middle of severe persecution from the anti-Christ and his system of government that is intent on torturing and killing as many Christians as possible, can you imagine their anger toward those who taught them that they wouldn't be here at this time? They will then be faced with making the decision to either accept or reject the "mark of the beast".

You might say that no one in their right mind would accept that mark, but remember that God will send a strong delusion so that those who love unrighteousness rather than the truth will believe the great lie that is presented by the anti-Christ and his cohorts.

2 Thessalonians 2:11, 12 And for this cause God shall send them strong delusion, that they should believe a lie: That they all might be damned who believed not the truth, but had pleasure in unrighteousness.

Also consider those who have taken the prosperity message to extremes and the

big-faith saints who believe that they will never suffer any real discomfort in their service to the Lord. I do not mean to

THE RAPTURE: DETAILS OF THE SECOND COMING OF CHRIST

depreciate true faith at all. As a matter of fact, it will require a tremendous amount of faith to make it through the difficult times that are ahead of us. We should consider the prophets and apostles as an example of suffering as the Scriptures instruct us.

There are some in the Church today who place material wealth and prosperity above service to Christ and as such are classified as idolaters according to the Scriptures.

Colossians 3:5 Mortify therefore your members which are upon the earth; fornication, uncleanness, inordinate affection, evil concupiscence, and covetousness, which is idolatry:

For those who are covetous, there is the hazard of disregarding the danger signals that are recorded in the Scriptures concerning the mark of the beast and running headlong toward the lake of fire that burns with fire and brimstone, which is the punishment for all who receive the mark of the beast or the number of his name.

Revelations 14:9-11 And the third angel followed them, saying with a loud voice, If any man worship the beast and his image, and receive his mark in his forehead, or in his hand, The same shall drink of the wine of the wrath of God, which is poured out without mixture into the cup of his indignation; and he shall be tormented with fire and brimstone in the presence of the holy angels, and in the presence of the Lamb: And the smoke of their torment ascendeth up for ever and ever: and they have no rest day nor night, who worship the beast and his image, and whosoever receiveth the mark of his name.

Truly today is the day to settle it in our hearts where we are in the Lord and just how far we are willing to follow Him.

For all those who have a problem giving themselves fully to the Lord now, it may be much harder to do in that day and with eternal consequences. Those who keep saying Christ is returning in 2000 etc. need to stop setting dates for the rapture.

THE RAPTURE: DETAILS OF THE SECOND COMING OF CHRIST

The Great Tribulation

The "Great Tribulation" referred to in the Bible is a time of trouble spoken of in both the Old and New Testaments as the greatest period of trouble ever experienced by Israel and the Church. It is referred to as "Jacob's trouble" and as the "great tribulation." Because it is referred to as Jacob's trouble, some Christians believe that it only applies to the Jews. We will look at the scriptural references to see who all is affected by this time of great persecution.

Revelations 13:3-17 And I saw one of his heads as it were wounded to death; and his deadly wound was healed: and all the world wondered after the beast. And they worshipped the dragon which gave power unto the beast: and they worshipped the beast, saying, Who is like unto the beast? who is able to make war with him? And there was given unto him a mouth speaking great things and blasphemies; and power was given unto him to continue forty and two months. And he opened his mouth in blasphemy against God, to blaspheme his name, and his tabernacle, and them that dwell in heaven. And it was given unto him to make war with the saints, and to overcome them: and power was given him over all kindreds, and tongues, and nations. And all that dwell upon the earth shall worship him, whose names are not written in the book of life of the Lamb slain from the foundation of the world. If any man have an ear, let him hear. He that leadeth into captivity shall go into captivity: he that killeth with the sword must be killed with the sword. Here is the patience and the faith of the saints. And I beheld another beast coming up out of the earth; and he had two horns like a lamb, and he spake as a dragon. And he exerciseth all the power of the first beast before him, and causeth the earth and them which dwell therein to worship the first beast, whose deadly wound was healed. And he doeth great wonders, so that he maketh fire come down from heaven on the earth in the sight of men, And deceiveth them that dwell on the earth by the means of those miracles which he had power to do in the sight of the beast; saying to them that dwell on the earth, that they should make an image to the beast, which had the wound by a sword, and did live. And he had power to give life unto the image of the beast, that the image of the beast should both speak, and cause that as many as would not worship the image of the beast should be killed. And he causeth all, both small and great, rich and poor, free and bond, to receive a mark in their right hand, or in their foreheads: And that no man might buy or sell, save he that had the mark, or the name of the beast, or the number of his name.

The word "saints" means exactly what it says. The reason there are saints on the earth during the time of the great tribulation is simple. There has been no resurrection of the dead, nor has there been a rapture. One of the reasons given for the Church being absent during the great tribulation by the pre-tribulation teachers is that the great tribulation is the wrath of God and we have not been appointed unto wrath.

THE GREAT TRIBULATION IS NOT THE WRATH OF GOD!

To say that the great tribulation is the wrath of God is completely without value. The Bible does mention the wrath of the devil and does specify a specific period of time which is three-and-one-half years.

THE RAPTURE: DETAILS OF THE SECOND COMING OF CHRIST

Revelations 12:7-17 And there was war in heaven: Michael and his angels fought against the dragon; and the dragon fought and his angels, And prevailed not; neither was their place found any more in heaven. And the great dragon was cast out, that old serpent, called the Devil, and Satan, which deceiveth the whole world: he was cast out into the earth, and his angels were cast out with him. And I heard a loud voice saying in heaven, Now is come salvation, and strength, and the kingdom of our God, and the power of his Christ: for the accuser of our brethren is cast down, which accused them before our God day and night. And they overcame him by the blood of the Lamb, and by the word of their testimony; and they loved not their lives unto the death. Therefore rejoice, ye heavens, and ye that dwell in them. Woe to the inhabiters of the earth and of the sea! for the devil is come down unto you, having great wrath, because he knoweth that he hath but a short time. And when the dragon saw that he was cast unto the earth, he persecuted the woman which brought forth the man child. And to the woman were given two wings of a great eagle, that she might fly into the wilderness, into her place, where she is nourished for a time, and times, and half a time, from the face of the serpent. And the serpent cast out of his mouth water as a flood after the woman, that he might cause her to be carried away of the flood. And the earth helped the woman, and the earth opened her mouth, and swallowed up the flood which the dragon cast out of his mouth. And the dragon was wroth with the woman, and went to make war with the remnant of her seed, which keep the commandments of God, and have the testimony of Jesus Christ.

The "remnant of her seed, which keep the commandments of God and have the testimony of Jesus Christ", is a clear reference to the Church. Nowhere in the Scriptures can we find that the great tribulation is the wrath of God. During the time of God's wrath, the Scriptures declare that God alone will be exalted.

Isaiah 2:10-12 Enter into the rock, and hide thee in the dust, for fear of the LORD, and for the glory of his majesty. The lofty looks of man shall be humbled, and the haughtiness of men shall be bowed down, and the LORD alone shall be exalted in that day. For the day of the LORD of hosts shall be upon every one that is proud and lofty, and upon every one that is lifted up; and he shall be brought low:

In the time of the great tribulation the anti-Christ will be ruling over all "kindred's, tongues and nations" and he will be exalted over all the people of the earth at that time. However, in the day of God's wrath, only God will be exalted. God and the anti-Christ cannot both be exalted at the same time.

WHAT DID JESUS SAY ABOUT THE GREAT TRIBULATION?

It is so important to look closely at Jesus' teachings concerning the rapture, the great tribulation and other end-time events. If we would follow this simple principle we would avoid a lot of error and sometimes downright nonsense. When Jesus was asked by His disciples about His return, he began by cautioning them against being deceived. He even said that many false prophets would arise for the specific purpose of deceiving many. He then began to give them a sequence of events (signs) that would precede His coming. Concerning the great tribulation, He said this;

THE RAPTURE: DETAILS OF THE SECOND COMING OF CHRIST

Matthew 24:15-21 When ye therefore shall see the abomination of desolation, spoken of by Daniel the prophet, stand in the holy place, (whoso readeth, let him understand:) Then let them which be in Judaea flee into the mountains: Let him which is on the housetop not come down to take any thing out of his house: Neither let him which is in the field return back to take his clothes. And woe unto them that are with child, and to them that give suck in those days! But pray ye that your flight be not in the winter, neither on the sabbath day: For then shall be great tribulation, such as was not since the beginning of the world to this time, no, nor ever shall be.

Jesus associates the beginning of the great tribulation with an event referred to as "the abomination of desolation" which was spoken of by Daniel, the prophet. Referring back to the book of Daniel, we find the reference to the abomination of desolation in Daniel 9:27.

Daniel 9:27 And he shall confirm the covenant with many for one week: and in the midst of the week he shall cause the sacrifice and the oblation to cease, and for the overspreading of abominations he shall make it desolate, even until the consummation, and that determined shall be poured upon the desolate.

(7 yrs.) and in the midst of the week (3 1/2 yrs. later) he shall cause the sacrifice to cease and for the overspreading of abominations he shall make it desolate, (the abomination of desolation) even until the consummation and that determined shall be poured upon the desolate.

And in Daniel 12 we see the same time frame for the great tribulation, which is 3 1/2 yrs.

Daniel 12:1-7 And at that time shall Michael stand up, the great prince which standeth for the children of thy people: and there shall be a time of trouble, such as never was since there was a nation even to that same time: and at that time thy people shall be delivered, every one that shall be found written in the book. And many of them that sleep in the dust of the earth shall awake, some to everlasting life, and some to shame and everlasting contempt. And they that be wise shall shine as the brightness of the firmament; and they that turn many to righteousness as the stars for ever and ever. But thou, O Daniel, shut up the words, and seal the book, even to the time of the end: many shall run to and fro, and knowledge shall be increased. Then I Daniel looked, and, behold, there stood other two, the one on this side of the bank of the river, and the other on that side of the bank of the river. And one said to the man clothed in linen, which was upon the waters of the river, How long shall it be to the end of these wonders? And I heard the man clothed in linen, which was upon the waters of the river, when he held up his right hand and his left hand unto heaven, and sware by him that liveth for ever that it shall be for a time, times, and an half; and when he shall have accomplished to scatter the power of the holy people, all these things shall be finished.

We must then, agree with the Scriptures that the great tribulation does not even begin until the middle of the seventieth week of Daniel, three and one-half years after the signing of the covenant referred to in Daniel 9:27. To try to make the Scriptures say something else is like trying to grasp thin air.

We can and should believe what the Scriptures teach clearly and not try to make it say something else.

THE CHURCH IS INCLUDED IN THE GREAT TRIBULATION

The pre-tribulation doctrine attempts to have the Church raptured before the great tribulation, which is in their opinion, at the beginning of the Seventieth Week of Daniel.

However, if we again look at the teachings of Jesus and the holy apostles and prophets, we must conclude that the Bible is very clear on this issue. When asked by His disciples when He would come again, Jesus spoke very clearly;

Matthew 24:29-31 Immediately after the tribulation of those days shall the sun be darkened, and the moon shall not give her light, and the stars shall fall from heaven, and the powers of the heavens shall be shaken: And then shall appear the sign of the Son of man in heaven: and then shall all the tribes of the earth mourn, and they shall see the Son of man coming in the clouds of heaven with power and great glory. And he shall send his angels with a great sound of a trumpet, and they shall gather together his elect from the four winds, from one end of heaven to the other.

Jesus very plainly stated that the rapture (the gathering together of His elect) would not occur until AFTER the tribulation of those days. Also, as we will see later in more detail, the above mentioned events, the sun being darkened, the moon not giving its light, the stars falling from heaven and the powers in heaven being shaken, ALL occur PRIOR to the rapture and the wrath of God. To say then, that the great tribulation is the wrath of God is totally unfounded in the Scriptures. This belief that the great tribulation is the wrath of God has caused many to error doctrinally concerning the doctrine of the rapture.

Because of this error that is the foundation of the pre-tribulation doctrine, everything else in the Scriptures is forced to fit the foundational error. What happens is that error after error is forced to fit the foundational error and the entire doctrine is corrupted. The Bible states very plainly that the Church will be on the earth during the great tribulation.

Revelations 7:9-14 After this I beheld, and, lo, a great multitude, which no man could number, of all nations, and kindreds, and people, and tongues, stood before the throne, and before the Lamb, clothed with white robes, and palms in their hands; And cried with a loud voice, saying, Salvation to our God which sitteth upon the throne, and unto the Lamb. And all the angels stood round about the throne, and about the elders and the four beasts, and fell before the throne on their faces, and worshipped God, Saying, Amen: Blessing, and glory, and wisdom, and thanksgiving, and honour, and power, and might, be unto our God for ever and ever. Amen. And one of the elders answered, saying unto me, What are these which are arrayed in white robes? and whence came they? And I said unto him, Sir, thou knowest. And he said to me, These are they which came out of great tribulation, and have washed their robes, and made them white in the blood of the Lamb.

Notice that those who came out of the great tribulation were a great multitude which could not be numbered and came out of all nations, kindreds and tongues. To say that these saints came out of the wrath of God is really stretching the Scriptures beyond comprehension. The Scriptures declare that those who suffered the wrath of God did not repent of their ungodliness, but rather cursed God to His face.

Revelations 16:8-11 And the fourth angel poured out his vial upon the sun; and power was given unto him to scorch men with fire. And men were scorched with great heat, and blasphemed the name of God, which hath power over these plagues: and they repented not to give him glory. And the fifth angel poured out his vial upon the seat of the beast; and his kingdom was full of darkness; and they gnawed their tongues for pain, And blasphemed the God of heaven because of their pains and their sores, and repented not of their deeds.

We must remember that during the wrath of God, Almighty God is pouring out His wrath full measure on an unrepentant ungodly people all over the world who have totally rejected Him. Of course the Church is not the object of His wrath and is not the recipient of the wrath of God. By this time the Church has been raptured and is that great multitude that stands before the throne and before the lamb. The Church is those who came out of great tribulation. NO one will be saved during the wrath of God.

Remember that Jesus said that His coming would be like the days of Noah and like the days of Lot. From this we can rightly conclude that the wrath of God will be poured out on the same day the Church is raptured.

Beloved, ask yourself this all important question; was it possible for anyone to be saved after the door was shut on the ark and the floods came? Likewise, was it possible for anyone to be saved after Lot and his family left Sodom? The obvious answer is no! Please consider this most important question and take the necessary steps today to prepare spiritually for the troublesome times ahead and to be certain that your family members and friends hear and receive the message of the gospel of Jesus Christ. To claim that the great tribulation is the wrath of God is without biblical merit.

THE WRATH OF GOD DOES NOT BEGIN UNTIL AFTER THE GREAT TRIBULATION AND THE RAPTURE

Revelations 8:1-6 And when he had opened the seventh seal, there was silence in heaven about the space of half an hour. And I saw the seven angels which stood before God; and to them were given seven trumpets. And another angel came and stood at the altar, having a golden censer; and there was given unto him much incense, that he should offer it with the prayers of all saints upon the golden altar which was before the throne. And the smoke of the incense, which came with the prayers of the saints, ascended up before God out of the angel's hand. And the angel took the censer, and filled it with fire of the altar, and cast it into the earth: and there were voices, and thunderings, and lightnings, and an earthquake. And the seven angels which had the seven trumpets prepared themselves to sound.

The wrath of God is announced at the sixth seal and the heavens convulse in anticipation of the wrath of God. Pre-tribulation teachers are right about the fact that we will not be here during God's wrath. The problem is that they confuse the great tribulation with God's wrath.

Revelations 6:12-17 And I beheld when he had opened the sixth seal, and, lo, there was a great earthquake; and the sun became black as sackcloth of hair, and the moon became as blood; And the stars of heaven fell unto the earth, even as a fig tree casteth her untimely figs, when she is shaken of a mighty wind. And the heaven departed as a scroll when it is rolled together; and every mountain and island were moved out of their places. And the kings of the earth, and the great men, and the rich men, and the chief captains, and the mighty men, and every bondman, and every free man, hid themselves in the dens and in the rocks of the mountains; And said to the mountains and rocks, Fall on us, and hide us from the face of him that sitteth on the throne, and from the wrath of the Lamb: For the great day of his wrath is come; and who shall be able to stand?

Jesus very clearly showed us that God's wrath and the rapture were to occur on the same day. Since there are signs to be observed prior to the wrath of God, these same signs will precede the rapture of the Church.

Matthew 24:29-31 Immediately after the tribulation of those days shall the sun be darkened, and the moon shall not give her light, and the stars shall fall from heaven, and the powers of the heavens shall be shaken: And then shall appear the sign of the Son of man in heaven: and then shall all the tribes of the earth mourn, and they shall see the Son of man coming in the clouds of heaven with power and great glory. And he shall send his angels with a great sound of a trumpet, and they shall gather together his elect from the four winds, from one end of heaven to the other.

Pre-tribulation rapture doctrine also teaches that the seals are the wrath of God. If this is true, why then do the souls under the altar at the fifth seal cry out to God to avenge them on their enemies?

Revelations 6:9-11 And when he had opened the fifth seal, I saw under the altar the souls of them that were slain for the word of God, and for the testimony which they held:

(10) And they cried with a loud voice, saying, How long, O Lord, holy and true, dost thou not judge and avenge our blood on them that dwell on the earth? And white robes were given unto every one of them; and it was said unto them, that they should rest yet for a little season, until their fellowservants also and their brethren, that should be killed as they were, should be fulfilled.

We can clearly see here that the wrath of God had not yet been initiated. How then can anyone say that it had? To do so clearly contradicts the teachings of the Holy Scriptures.

THE RAPTURE: DETAILS OF THE SECOND COMING OF CHRIST

These Events Must Precede the Rapture

THE ANTI-CHRIST MUST FIRST BE ESTABLISHED

In Paul's letter to the Thessalonians, he gave them instruction concerning the rapture, or as he put it, "our gathering together unto Him." If we would use this scriptural terminology rather than the Latin word "rapture," we would be better able to understand this great event. When viewing the rapture using biblical language, it is easy to understand what Jesus said about the gathering together of His elect at the end of the age. In plain language Jesus told His disciples when the rapture would occur.

If we will stick with what is being said in the Scriptures and not deviate from the word, we will be better able to understand biblical doctrine.

Matthew 24:29-31 Immediately after the tribulation of those days shall the sun be darkened, and the moon shall not give her light, and the stars shall fall from heaven, and the powers of the heavens shall be shaken: And then shall appear the sign of the Son of man in heaven: and then shall all the tribes of the earth mourn, and they shall see the Son of man coming in the clouds of heaven with power and great glory. And he shall send his angels with a great sound of a trumpet, and they shall gather together his elect from the four winds, from one end of heaven to the other.

Paul also told the saints that there would be some definite things to watch for prior to the rapture. Paul's purpose in writing to the Church was to correct some doctrinal error that had been taught by possible prophetic utterance, by false teachings and perhaps some who had even forged a letter in Paul's, or one of his companions names. His concern was that they were being deceived by false teachers who were propagating false doctrine. Notice that Paul specifically refers to the coming of the Lord AND "our gathering together unto Him." Please note that Paul mentions the coming of Christ BEFORE the gathering together. This sequence of events agrees perfectly with Jesus' teaching in Matthew 24, where He said the world would see Him COMING in the clouds and then He would "gather together" His elect.

2 Thessalonians 2:1 Now we beseech you, brethren, by the coming of our Lord Jesus Christ, and by our gathering together unto him,

Matthew 24:30, 31 And then shall appear the sign of the Son of man in heaven: and then shall all the tribes of the earth mourn, and they shall see the Son of man coming in the clouds of heaven with power and great glory. And he shall send his angels with a great sound of a trumpet, and they shall gather together his elect from the four winds, from one end of heaven to the other.

To reverse this order of events, which the pre-tribulation doctrine clearly does, is to oppose the teachings of Jesus Christ and the apostle Paul. The pre-tribulation teaching emphatically states that the gathering together precedes the coming of Christ. You be the judge, who will you believe? Will you trust in the clear order of events stated in the Scriptures by Jesus and Paul, or will you believe a doctrine that so clearly denies the truth of Scripture? Please take a moment and think about this order of events. Jesus and Paul both teach that the coming is before the gathering together.

To teach anything else is clearly denying the Lord Jesus and Paul, the apostle of Christ who received first hand revelation concerning these events.

2 Thessalonians 2:1-5 Now we beseech you, brethren, by the coming of our Lord Jesus Christ, and by our gathering together unto him, That ye be not soon shaken in mind, or be troubled, neither by spirit, nor by word, nor by letter as from us, as that the day of Christ is at hand. Let no man deceive you by any means: for that day shall not come, except there come a falling away first, and that man of sin be revealed, the son of perdition; Who opposeth and exalteth himself above all that is called God, or that is worshipped; so that he as God sitteth in the temple of God, shewing himself that he is God. Remember ye not, that, when I was yet with you, I told you these things?

Paul specifically warned the saints in Thessalonica of being deceived. Any time the Scriptures speak about the possibility of being deceived we should pay special attention to what is being said.

There are two definite events spoken of by Paul that absolutely must take place before the "Day of Christ" occurs.

1. There must be a falling away first.

The phrase "falling away" literally means a defection from the truth. Paul said it this way in writing to Timothy;

1 Timothy 4:1 Now the Spirit speaketh expressly, that in the latter times some shall depart from the faith, giving heed to seducing spirits, and doctrines of devils;

Those that will depart from the faith in that day will be those that have been in the faith. The Bible says that the last days will be perilous times. Jesus said that even the very elect might be deceived.

Mark 13:22 For false Christs and false prophets shall rise, and shall shew signs and wonders, to seduce, if it were possible, even the elect.

2. The anti-Christ must be revealed who will sit in the temple of God, demanding to be worshipped as God and showing himself that he IS God. This man will proclaim himself to be God and anyone who will not worship him will be persecuted and many will be killed. The Bible tells us when the anti-Christ will be established in his time of rule over all the earth. Jesus said that when we see the abomination of desolation spoken of by Daniel the prophet stand in the holy place, that then the Great Tribulation would begin.

Matthew 24:15 When ye therefore shall see the abomination of desolation, spoken of by Daniel the prophet, stand in the holy place, (whoso readeth, let him understand:)

Matthew 24:21 For then shall be great tribulation, such as was not since the beginning of the world to this time, no, nor ever shall be.

Jesus is referring to Daniel 9:27 that shows clearly that this event occurs in the middle of the week, or three and one-half years after the beginning of the Seventieth Week of Daniel.

Daniel 9:27 And he shall confirm the covenant with many for one week: and in the midst of the week he shall cause the sacrifice and the oblation to cease, and for the overspreading of abominations he shall make it desolate, even until the consummation, and that determined shall be poured upon the desolate.

THE RAPTURE: DETAILS OF THE SECOND COMING OF CHRIST

Jesus cannot come until at least the middle of Daniel's seventieth week. But we know according to Jesus' own words that He is coming to gather together His saints "immediately after the tribulation of those days."

THE GOSPEL MUST BE PREACHED IN ALL THE WORLD

Another important event that must take place is the preaching of the gospel to the entire world. Although the gospel has been preached in many nations, the gospel has not yet been preached to all the world.

Matthew 24:14 And this gospel of the kingdom shall be preached in all the world for a witness unto all nations; and then shall the end come.

Revelations 14:1-20 And I looked, and, lo, a Lamb stood on the mount Sion, and with him an hundred forty and four thousand, having his Father's name written in their foreheads. And I heard a voice from heaven, as the voice of many waters, and as the voice of a great thunder: and I heard the voice of harpers harping with their harps: And they sung as it were a new song before the throne, and before the four beasts, and the elders: and no man could learn that song but the hundred and forty and four thousand, which were redeemed from the earth. These are they which were not defiled with women; for they are virgins. These are they which follow the Lamb whithersoever he goeth. These were redeemed from among men, being the firstfruits unto God and to the Lamb. And in their mouth was found no guile: for they are without fault before the throne of God. And I saw another angel fly in the midst of heaven, having the everlasting gospel to preach unto them that dwell on the earth, and to every nation, and kindred, and tongue, and people, Saying with a loud voice, Fear God, and give glory to him; for the hour of his judgment is come: and worship him that made heaven, and earth, and the sea, and the fountains of waters. And there followed another angel, saying, Babylon is fallen, is fallen, that great city, because she made all nations drink of the wine of the wrath of her fornication. And the third angel followed them, saying with a loud voice, If any man worship the beast and his image, and receive his mark in his forehead, or in his hand, The same shall drink of the wine of the wrath of God, which is poured out without mixture into the cup of his indignation; and he shall be tormented with fire and brimstone in the presence of the holy angels, and in the presence of the Lamb: And the smoke of their torment ascendeth up for ever and ever: and they have no rest day nor night, who worship the beast and his image, and whosoever receiveth the mark of his name. Here is the patience of the saints: here are they that keep the commandments of God, and the faith of Jesus. And I heard a voice from heaven saying unto me, Write, Blessed are the dead which die in the Lord from henceforth: Yea, saith the Spirit, that they may rest from their labours; and their works do follow them. And I looked, and behold a white cloud, and upon the cloud one sat like unto the Son of man, having on his head a golden crown, and in his hand a sharp sickle. And another angel came out of the temple, crying with a loud voice to him that sat on the cloud, Thrust in thy sickle, and reap: for the time is come for thee to reap; for the harvest of the earth is ripe. And he that sat on the cloud thrust in his sickle on the earth; and the earth was reaped. And another angel came out of the temple which is in heaven, he also having a sharp sickle. And another angel came out from

THE RAPTURE: DETAILS OF THE SECOND COMING OF CHRIST

the altar, which had power over fire; and cried with a loud cry to him that had the sharp sickle, saying, Thrust in thy sharp sickle, and gather the clusters of the vine of the earth; for her grapes are fully ripe. And the angel thrust in his sickle into the earth, and gathered the vine of the earth, and cast it into the great winepress of the wrath of God. And the winepress was trodden without the city, and blood came out of the winepress, even unto the horse bridles, by the space of a thousand and six hundred furlongs.

Revelations 15:1 And I saw another sign in heaven, great and marvellous, seven angels having the seven last plagues; for in them is filled up the wrath of God.

The sequence of events mentioned in the above verses of Scripture must not be overlooked, nor should we disregard the perfect succession of the occurrence of each event.

First of all, we see Jesus with the 144,000 Jews who were redeemed among men from the earth, being the first fruits unto God and unto the Lamb.

Revelations 7:2-5 And I saw another angel ascending from the east, having the seal of the living God: and he cried with a loud voice to the four angels, to whom it was given to hurt the earth and the sea, Saying, Hurt not the earth, neither the sea, nor the trees, till we have sealed the servants of our God in their foreheads. And I heard the number of them which were sealed: and there were sealed an hundred and forty and four thousand of all the tribes of the children of Israel. Of the tribe of Juda were sealed twelve thousand. Of the tribe of Reuben were sealed twelve thousand. Of the tribe of Gad were sealed twelve thousand.

It is so important to note that the wrath of God does not begin until the 144,000 are sealed which occurs at the seventh seal.

The wrath of God is mentioned in the sixth seal and begins to be poured out at the opening of the seventh seal. Prior to the sixth seal all the events of the first five seals had already taken place. The wrath of God is about to be poured out. Since we know we have not been appointed unto wrath, we know that we will not experience that event. However, the wrath of God has not been poured out at the beginning of the Seventieth Week of Daniel as pre-tribulation teaches, because the Great Tribulation does not last for seven years, as is commonly taught. Jesus stated that the Great Tribulation would not begin until the middle of the week when He quoted from the book of Daniel. Who are we going to believe? The seventh seal deals with the events that take place after the Church is raptured immediately after the tribulation of those days exactly as Jesus had said to his disciples. Next we see the angel proclaiming the everlasting gospel to preach to every nation, kindred and tongue. Jesus said that this would be the last thing to take place before the end would come.

The angel also gives a warning to all not to take the mark of the beast and warns every one of the consequences of doing so.

Revelations 14:9-11 And the third angel followed them, saying with a loud voice, If any man worship the beast and his image, and receive his mark in his forehead, or in his hand, The same shall drink of the wine of the wrath of God, which is poured out without mixture into the cup of his indignation; and he shall be tormented with fire and brimstone in the presence of the holy angels, and in the presence of the Lamb:

THE RAPTURE: DETAILS OF THE SECOND COMING OF CHRIST

And the smoke of their torment ascendeth up for ever and ever: and they have no rest day nor night, who worship the beast and his image, and whosoever receiveth the mark of his name.

Next we see that there will be some who will die in the Lord from that moment on. It is safe to assume that those will be Christians. Then we see that Jesus thrusts His sickle into the earth and the earth is reaped, which is "our gathering together unto Him."

We are not told how much time expires between those who die in the Lord during the time of the Great Tribulation and the rapture, but Jesus said that those days would be cut short.

Matthew 24:22 And except those days should be shortened, there should no flesh be saved: but for the elect's sake those days shall be shortened.

The next event that occurs is the angel who thrusts his sickle into the earth and gathered the vine of the earth and cast it into the great winepress of the wrath of God. This begins the outpouring of God's wrath upon an ungodly, unrepentant world. Then we see the seven angels having the seven last plagues which complete the wrath of God.

THE MOON MUST TURN TO BLOOD

For those who say there are no prophecies to be fulfilled before the rapture, please consider this;

Matthew 24:29-31 Immediately after the tribulation of those days shall the sun be darkened, and the moon shall not give her light, and the stars shall fall from heaven, and the powers of the heavens shall be shaken: And then shall appear the sign of the Son of man in heaven: and then shall all the tribes of the earth mourn, and they shall see the Son of man coming in the clouds of heaven with power and great glory. And he shall send his angels with a great sound of a trumpet, and they shall gather together his elect from the four winds, from one end of heaven to the other.

PEOPLE GET READY JESUS IS COMING.
WE DON'T KNOW WHEN, BUT WE DO HAVE SIGNS WE ARE CLOSER.
IT'S TIME TO BECOME THAT GLORIOUS CHURCH AND WORK TOGETHER TO SEE THE GREATEST MOVE OF GOD OF ALL TIME!

THE RAPTURE: DETAILS OF THE SECOND COMING OF CHRIST

This is the Day of the Lord

The day of the Lord is referenced often in the Scriptures and we are given a detailed account of this event. There are many things that happen in the day of the Lord. I am going to release some prophetic pictures concerning the United States throughout this book. Following is a list of Scripture verses that refer to the day of the Lord.

Isaiah 2:11-17 The lofty looks of man shall be humbled, and the haughtiness of men shall be bowed down, and the LORD alone shall be exalted in that day. For the day of the LORD of hosts *shall be* upon every *one that is* proud and lofty, and upon every *one that is* lifted up; and he shall be brought low: And upon all the cedars of Lebanon, *that are* high and lifted up, and upon all the oaks of Bashan, And upon all the high mountains, and upon all the hills *that are* lifted up, And upon every high tower, and upon every fenced wall, And upon all the ships of Tarshish, and upon all pleasant pictures. And the loftiness of man shall be bowed down, and the haughtiness of men shall be made low: and the LORD alone shall be exalted in that day. Howl ye; for the day of the LORD *is* at hand; it shall come as a destruction from the Almighty. Therefore shall all hands be faint, and every man's heart shall melt: And they shall be afraid: pangs and sorrows shall take hold of them; they shall be in pain as a woman that travaileth: they shall be amazed one at another; their faces *shall be as* flames. Behold, the day of the LORD cometh, cruel both with wrath and fierce anger, to lay the land desolate: and he shall destroy the sinners thereof out of it. For the stars of heaven and the constellations thereof shall not give their light: the sun shall be darkened in his going forth, and the moon shall not cause her light to shine. And I will punish the world for *their* evil, and the wicked for their iniquity; and I will cause the arrogancy of the proud to cease, and will lay low the haughtiness of the terrible. I will make a man more precious than fine gold; even a man than the golden wedge of Ophir. Therefore I will shake the heavens, and the earth shall remove out of her place, in the wrath of the LORD of hosts, and in the day of his fierce anger.

Jeremiah 46:10 For this *is* the day of the Lord GOD of hosts, a day of vengeance, that he may avenge him of his adversaries: and the sword shall devour, and it shall be satiate and made drunk with their blood: for the Lord GOD of hosts hath a sacrifice in the north country by the river Euphrates.

Ezekiel 30:1-3 The word of the LORD came again unto me, saying, Son of man, prophesy and say, Thus saith the Lord GOD; Howl ye, Woe worth the day! For the day *is* near, even the day of the LORD *is* near, a cloudy day; it shall be the time of the heathen.

Joel 1:15 Alas for the day! for the day of the LORD *is* at hand, and as a destruction from the Almighty shall it come.

Joel 2:1, 2 Blow ye the trumpet in Zion, and sound an alarm in my holy mountain: let all the inhabitants of the land tremble: for the day of the LORD cometh, for *it is* nigh at hand; A day of darkness and of gloominess, a day of clouds and of thick darkness, as the morning spread upon the mountains: a great people and a strong; there hath not been ever the like, neither shall be any more after it, *even* to the years of many generations.

Joel 2:31, 32 The sun shall be turned into darkness, and the moon into blood, before the great and the terrible day of the LORD come. And it shall come to pass, *that* whosoever shall

THE RAPTURE: DETAILS OF THE SECOND COMING OF CHRIST

call on the name of the LORD shall be delivered: for in mount Zion and in Jerusalem shall be deliverance, as the LORD hath said, and in the remnant whom the LORD shall call.

Joel 3:13-15 Put ye in the sickle, for the harvest is ripe: come, get you down; for the press is full, the fats overflow; for their wickedness *is* great. Multitudes, multitudes in the valley of decision: for the day of the LORD *is* near in the valley of decision. The sun and the moon shall be darkened, and the stars shall withdraw their shining.

Amos 5:18-20 Woe unto you that desire the day of the LORD! to what end *is* it for you? the day of the LORD *is* darkness, and not light. As if a man did flee from a lion, and a bear met him; or went into the house, and leaned his hand on the wall, and a serpent bit him. *Shall* not the day of the LORD *be* darkness, and not light? even very dark, and no brightness in it?

Zephaniah 1:14-18 The great day of the LORD *is* near, *it is* near, and hasteth greatly, *even* the voice of the day of the LORD: the mighty man shall cry there bitterly. That day *is* a day of wrath, a day of trouble and distress, a day of wasteness and desolation, a day of darkness and gloominess, a day of clouds and thick darkness, A day of the trumpet and alarm against the fenced cities, and against the high towers. And I will bring distress upon men, that they shall walk like blind men, because they have sinned against the LORD: and their blood shall be poured out as dust, and their flesh as the dung. Neither their silver nor their gold shall be able to deliver them in the day of the LORD'S wrath; but the whole land shall be devoured by the fire of his jealousy: for he shall make even a speedy riddance of all them that dwell in the land.

1 Thessalonians 5:1-9 But of the times and the seasons, brethren, ye have no need that I write unto you. For yourselves know perfectly that the day of the Lord so cometh as a thief in the night. For when they shall say, Peace and safety; then sudden destruction cometh upon them, as travail upon a woman with child; and they shall not escape. But ye, brethren, are not in darkness, that that day should overtake you as a thief. Ye are all the children of light, and the children of the day: we are not of the night, nor of darkness. Therefore let us not sleep, as *do* others; but let us watch and be sober. For they that sleep sleep in the night; and they that be drunken are drunken in the night. But let us, who are of the day, be sober, putting on the breastplate of faith and love; and for an helmet, the hope of salvation. For God hath not appointed us to wrath, but to obtain salvation by our Lord Jesus Christ,

The day of the Lord is an awesome time of God's wrath being poured out upon a stubborn, unrepentant people who are like the people in Noah's day whose wickedness caused God to pour out his wrath upon them.

Genesis 6:5-7 And GOD saw that the wickedness of man *was* great in the earth, and *that* every imagination of the thoughts of his heart *was* only evil continually. And it repented the LORD that he had made man on the earth, and it grieved him at his heart. And the LORD said, I will destroy man whom I have created from the face of the earth; both man, and beast, and the creeping thing, and the fowls of the air; for it repenteth me that I have made them.

The days of Lot were filled with men whose sin had reached up to heaven and demanded the wrath of God to be poured out upon their wickedness.

THE RAPTURE: DETAILS OF THE SECOND COMING OF CHRIST

Genesis 13:13 But the men of Sodom *were* wicked and sinners before the LORD exceedingly.

If we compare this present day we are living in, we can easily see that the wickedness of men is great, just as it was in Noah and Lot's days. Sexual sin and perversion is viewed in our nation and in most nations of the world as an acceptable, alternate lifestyle. Presidents of America Obama and Clinton and their wives have done much to promote homosexuality and lesbianism as acceptable lifestyles in this nation. They have promoted abortion all over the world as an acceptable means of birth control. There has been the creation of a day after sex pill. This is giving sexual active teens and adults a way to have unsafe sex and then take a pill not to get pregnant. Abortion didn't begin with the Clintons, but it has reached a horrible pinnacle in partial-birth abortion which is the murder of partially delivered babies. Legislation was introduced that would ban partial-birth abortion, but it was voted in by President Clinton. There can be no doubt where Clinton and other liberal politicians stand on the issue of abortion, homosexuality, lesbianism, and disgusting sexual perversion. This kind of ungodly leadership definitely brings consequences upon our nation. The life is literally sucked out of these precious little bodies by puncturing the baby's skull and sucking its brains out. Those who favor partial-birth abortion claim the babies feel no pain, but those doctors and nurses who have witnessed this method of murder tell a much different story. God sees every one of those little bodies while they struggle in pain as the life is being sucked out of them and their bodies dismembered. He also hears the cries of each one as they are being slaughtered in the name of the personal rights of the mothers who carried them. I am not speaking evil of the Presidents Obama and Clinton. I am simply stating facts that are a part of public record. The Bible says that righteousness exalts a nation, but sin is a reproach to many people. Surely Presidents and political leaders have brought a reproach upon our nation. How can anyone dare to think that God will not judge America for this abomination of the murder of innocent little babies? What does the Bible have to say about abortion, the murder of innocent little babies?

There are things like all of this that leads to cloning humans and some of the most twisted abominations to God.

I want to insert something here. Despite all the trouble that has come to our wonderful country God is still our provider. The financial fall to where we are in America doesn't have to affect us as Children of God.

Jeremiah 2:34, 35 Also in thy skirts is found the blood of the souls of the poor innocents: I have not found it by secret search, but upon all these. Yet thou sayest, Because I am innocent, surely his anger shall turn from me. Behold, I will plead with thee, because thou sayest, I have not sinned.

Jeremiah 5:9 Shall I not visit for these *things?* saith the LORD: and shall not my soul be avenged on such a nation as this?

There can be no doubt that the world has degenerated to the same sins that called for God's wrath in the past, and that the time of God's judgment is at hand again.

According to scriptures God's wrath does not occur until after the rapture of the Church has taken place, and that the rapture occurs "immediately after the tribulation of those days", according to Jesus. The day of the Lord is reserved for the unrepentant, godless, wicked people of the world who have totally rejected Christ and have chosen the way of wickedness, just as it was in the days of Noah when the wickedness of men was great. And just as God prepared an ark of safety for the righteous in Noah's day, He has also provided a means of escape for the righteous of our present time. That ark of safety is none other than the Lord Jesus Christ. The Bible refers to "gathering together", or as we commonly refer to it, the rapture. Saints of God will be spared from this awesome display of God's ultimate displeasure with the wicked and His judgment upon the earth.

Doctrine Errors

One of the Doctrines that have been taught in error is that Jesus could return at any moment. Since the doctrine that Jesus can return at any moment without any signs or any Bible prophecies that are yet to be fulfilled is a foundational stone of the pre-tribulation doctrine, let's examine that doctrine in light of Scripture, precept upon precept, line upon line.

It is commonly taught by pre-tribulation teachers that the apostles expected and taught that the return of Christ was possible, and that Jesus could return in their lifetime. It doesn't take long at all to prove this belief untrue according to scripture.

2 Peter 1:12-15 Wherefore I will not be negligent to put you always in remembrance of these things, though ye know *them,* and be established in the present truth. Yea, I think it meet, as long as I am in this tabernacle, to stir you up by putting *you* in remembrance; Knowing that shortly I must put off *this* my tabernacle, even as our Lord Jesus Christ hath shewed me. Moreover I will endeavour that ye may be able after my decease to have these things always in remembrance.

Peter very clearly stated that he would die before the return of Christ. He made reference to the prophetic word given to him by Jesus concerning his death.

John 21:17-19 He saith unto him the third time, Simon, *son* of Jonas, lovest thou me? Peter was grieved because he said unto him the third time, Lovest thou me? And he said unto him, Lord, thou knowest all things; thou knowest that I love thee. Jesus saith unto him, Feed my sheep. Verily, verily, I say unto thee, When thou wast young, thou girdedst thyself, and walkedst whither thou wouldest: but when thou shalt be old, thou shalt stretch forth thy hands, and another shall gird thee, and carry *thee* whither thou wouldest not. This spake he, signifying by what death he should glorify God. And when he had spoken this, he saith unto him, Follow me.

2 Timothy 4:6-8 For I am now ready to be offered, and the time of my departure is at hand. I have fought a good fight, I have finished *my* course, I have kept the faith: Henceforth there is laid up for me a crown of righteousness, which the Lord, the righteous judge, shall give me at that day: and not to me only, but unto all them also that love his appearing.

Paul didn't teach according to the Word the doctrine of imminence return of the Lord. The doctrine of imminence is so contrary to the teachings of Scriptures that it reminds us of Jesus and Paul's warning to us to not be deceived. We must see how unbiblical the pre-tribulation rapture is, so that we will not trust in this erroneous doctrine that is being taught to the Church in these last days.

Hebrews 11:35-40 Women received their dead raised to life again: and others were tortured, not accepting deliverance; that they might obtain a better resurrection: And others had trial of *cruel* mockings and scourgings, yea, moreover of bonds and imprisonment: They were stoned, they were sawn asunder, were tempted, were slain with the sword: they wandered about in sheepskins and goatskins; being destitute, afflicted, tormented; (Of whom the world was not worthy:) they wandered in deserts, and *in* mountains, and *in* dens and caves of the earth. And these all, having obtained a good report through faith, received not the promise: God having provided some better thing for us, that they without us should not be made perfect.

It is a blasphemous statement! How can anyone claim to have received revelation from the Lord when it is contrary to the Scriptures?

A serious problem with these preachers, who teach revelations from supposed visions and revelations in the spirit, is the fact that the spirits they are hearing from are in direct opposition to the standard of all revelation, the holy Bible. So, then, who are they hearing from? Revelation has to come and line up with scriptures. Are these "revelations" coming from the imagination and minds of men, or are they receiving revelation from demonic spirits who have appeared themselves as angels of light? A problem with many ministers today is the fact that they seem to be receiving "revelations" that are not in accordance with the Scriptures. Some are promoting visions and revelations that are in direct disagreement with the Bible. This has come with the extreme beliefs that get spooky and there are others whom are preaching there is no more power.

2 Timothy 4:1-4 I charge *thee* therefore before God, and the Lord Jesus Christ, who shall judge the quick and the dead at his appearing and his kingdom; Preach the word; be instant in season, out of season; reprove, rebuke, exhort with all longsuffering and doctrine. For the time will come when they will not endure sound doctrine; but after their own lusts shall they heap to themselves teachers, having itching ears; And they shall turn away *their* ears from the truth, and shall be turned unto fables.

There are Books and videos being offered today that show what will happen to those who are left behind when Jesus comes for His Church. They tell how those who are left behind will suffer persecution and tribulation at the hands of the

THE RAPTURE: DETAILS OF THE SECOND COMING OF CHRIST

anti-Christ, which they believe is the wrath of God. The problem with those who are left behind at the rapture is far more serious than being in the great tribulation. Those who do not go in the rapture are left behind to face the severe wrath of God, and cannot be saved during that time. This is one of the most dangerous aspects of the pre-tribulation doctrine. It is a deceiving, damnable doctrine slipped into the Church by the devil. The doctrine of the pre-tribulation rapture is, according to Scripture, a false doctrine. That does not mean that everyone who teaches this doctrine is a false teacher. I have several very good well meaning friends who believe in and teach the pre-tribulation doctrine. Our friendship is not based on our doctrinal beliefs, but rather on our mutual relationship with Jesus Christ, and the fact that we are family in Christ. I am very careful to guard my relationship with my brethren who believe the pre-tribulation doctrine. I am committed to them. I am not going to force feed them because that will just cause them not to receive. There are many within the Church preaching false things about divorce and once saved always saved. We all can lose our salvation if we choose not to turn away from sin. God hates divorce but I believe that repentance can come and that person can still become great for God and even remarry. This teaching that is out there is abandoning many within the Body of Christ because they have been divorced I will be writing a book specific to the topic of divorce soon. These are both false and those whom believe this are cramming it down believers with a wrong heart. Their heart is causing much discord within the Church.

The truth is that we are family, we are members of one another according to the Scriptures. I treasure my relationship will all my brethren I am in relationship with, and will do all I can to maintain a healthy relationship with them. The fact that we understand this doctrine differently is an indication that we are not hearing from the same spirit. Knowing this, it should compel us to come together and sit before the Holy Spirit together, so we can all come to the same conclusion concerning this doctrine. Some have just been taught false doctrine and need fresh revelation to awaken the truth.

I am certain that many Christian teachers, when confronted with the lack of scriptural foundation for the pre-tribulation doctrine, will re-evaluate their position, and go to the Scriptures for a true understanding of this doctrine. In no way am I trying to discredit any of my brethren in Christ who teach the pre-tribulation doctrine, but I am hoping to disprove this erroneous doctrine that is contrary to the Scriptures. Nor do I claim to have all the truth concerning the gathering together of the saints, but I will continue to expose this false doctrine while loving and respecting my brethren in Christ. There truly are some who have left the borders of the Scriptures, and are teaching false doctrine in order to fleece God's sheep. It is not my intention to lump all who teach the pre-tribulation doctrine in this category, but it must be stated that there are many ministers today that are doing just that. How can it be that Bible students who all love the Lord and His holy word come up with doctrines that are directly opposed to each other and still believe that individually we are all hearing from the Holy Spirit?

I believe that one of the most significant problems is the fact that some are trying to understand doctrine with their natural intellect rather than receiving revelation from the Holy

THE RAPTURE: DETAILS OF THE SECOND COMING OF CHRIST

Spirit. Jesus said that His words were spirit and life, and as such must be interpreted by the Spirit. No amount of carnal reasoning and logic can ever bring us into knowledge of the truths of Scripture. Our doctrine is also generally influenced by the particular "camp" we are associated with. In order to remain in good standing with our brethren in that camp, we are expected to agree with the doctrinal views by that group. It is hard to go against some of the most highly regarded and popular teachers of our day, and still remain in the religious "in crowd." The Bible tells us that the Holy Spirit is our teacher, and as such we should be able to understand that we all should be receiving the same revelations concerning the doctrine of the rapture, and that we all should be receiving the same revelations concerning the doctrine of the rapture, and other doctrines as well. While we are continuing to hold fast to our differing doctrines we are creating confusion within the body of Christ. If we as teachers cannot get our doctrine straight, how can we expect the rest of the body to? Isn't it time for teachers in the body to get it together? The Bible also tells us that the natural man (mind) cannot receive the things of God because they are foolishness to him.

1 Corinthians 2:14 But the natural man receiveth not the things of the Spirit of God: for they are foolishness unto him: neither can he know *them,* because they are spiritually discerned.

Now is the time to preach the gospel to your family and friends if you don't want them to spend forever in the lake of fire that burns with fire and brimstone. If your family members and friends don't go in the rapture, they will be left to suffer the wrath of God that is poured out without mixture. I don't mean the great tribulation, I am talking about the wrath of God which has nothing to do with the great tribulation. We need to love our friends and family with the Gospel of Jesus Christ.

The pre-tribulation doctrine teaches that it was always possible for Jesus to come at any moment and that there are no prophesied events in Scripture that had to be fulfilled before He could come. Could Jesus have come for the Church before Israel became a nation again? Could all of the prophesied events of the last days be fulfilled concerning Israel if they had not been restored as a nation? If the rapture could not have been imminent before Israel became a nation, how can it be imminent now? The doctrine of imminence has no foundation in the Scriptures, and is easily proven to be false doctrine. This is just one more strike against the pre-tribulation rapture doctrine, and should be recognized for what it is. When Paul taught about the coming of the Lord and the gathering together of His saints, he emphatically warned us about being deceived. Paul taught that Jesus would first come, and afterward gather together His elect. Please don't be deceived, these events will occur in the exact order that both Paul and Jesus taught. They both warned all who would hear not to believe anything other than that prescribed order of events!

The Return of Christ

The best way to learn about the end-times is to read the scriptures over and over again. We must allow the Holy Spirit to speak as we study the scriptures.

1 Corinthians 1:1-7 Paul, called *to be* an apostle of Jesus Christ through the will of God, and Sosthenes *our* brother, Unto the church of God which is at Corinth, to them that are sanctified in Christ Jesus, called *to be* saints, with all that in every place call upon the name of Jesus Christ our Lord, both theirs and ours: Grace *be* unto you, and peace, from God our Father, and *from* the Lord Jesus Christ. I thank my God always on your behalf, for the grace of God which is given you by Jesus Christ; That in every thing ye are enriched by him, in all utterance, and *in* all knowledge; Even as the testimony of Christ was confirmed in you: So that ye come behind in no gift; waiting for the coming of our Lord Jesus Christ:

1 Corinthians 15:20-26 But now is Christ risen from the dead, *and* become the firstfruits of them that slept. For since by man *came* death, by man *came* also the resurrection of the dead. For as in Adam all die, even so in Christ shall all be made alive. But every man in his own order: Christ the firstfruits; afterward they that are Christ's at his coming. Then *cometh* the end, when he shall have delivered up the kingdom to God, even the Father; when he shall have put down all rule and all authority and power. For he must reign, till he hath put all enemies under his feet. The last enemy *that* shall be destroyed *is* death.

1 Thessalonians 3:12, 13 And the Lord make you to increase and abound in love one toward another, and toward all *men,* even as we *do* toward you: To the end he may stablish your

hearts unblameable in holiness before God, even our Father, at the coming of our Lord Jesus Christ with all his saints.

1 Thessalonians 4:13-17 But I would not have you to be ignorant, brethren, concerning them which are asleep, that ye sorrow not, even as others which have no hope. For if we believe that Jesus died and rose again, even so them also which sleep in Jesus will God bring with him. For this we say unto you by the word of the Lord, that we which are alive *and* remain unto the coming of the Lord shall not prevent them which are asleep. For the Lord himself shall descend from heaven with a shout, with the voice of the archangel, and with the trump of God: and the dead in Christ shall rise first: Then we which are alive *and* remain shall be caught up together with them in the clouds, to meet the Lord in the air: and so shall we ever be with the Lord.

1 Thessalonians 5:23 And the very God of peace sanctify you wholly; and *I pray God* your whole spirit and soul and body be preserved blameless unto the coming of our Lord Jesus Christ.

2 Thessalonians 2:1 Now we beseech you, brethren, by the coming of our Lord Jesus Christ, and *by* our gathering together unto him, That ye be not soon shaken in mind, or be troubled, neither by spirit, nor by word, nor by letter as from us, as that the day of Christ is at hand.

James 5:7, 8 Be patient therefore, brethren, unto the coming of the Lord. Behold, the husbandman waiteth for the precious fruit of the earth, and hath long patience for it, until he receive the early and latter rain. Be ye also patient; stablish your hearts: for the coming of the Lord draweth nigh.

THE RAPTURE: DETAILS OF THE SECOND COMING OF CHRIST

2 Peter 3:10-14 But the day of the Lord will come as a thief in the night; in the which the heavens shall pass away with a great noise, and the elements shall melt with fervent heat, the earth also and the works that are therein shall be burned up. *Seeing* then *that* all these things shall be dissolved, what manner *of persons* ought ye to be in *all* holy conversation and godliness, Looking for and hasting unto the coming of the day of God, wherein the heavens being on fire shall be dissolved, and the elements shall melt with fervent heat? Nevertheless we, according to his promise, look for new heavens and a new earth, wherein dwelleth righteousness. Wherefore, beloved, seeing that ye look for such things, be diligent that ye may be found of him in peace, without spot, and blameless.

The Rapture and the wrath of God occur at the same time. Study the scriptures and you will see this.

Luke 17:26-30 And as it was in the days of Noe, so shall it be also in the days of the Son of man. They did eat, they drank, they married wives, they were given in marriage, until the day that Noe entered into the ark, and the flood came, and destroyed them all. Likewise also as it was in the days of Lot; they did eat, they drank, they bought, they sold, they planted, they builded; But the same day that Lot went out of Sodom it rained fire and brimstone from heaven, and destroyed *them* all. Even thus shall it be in the day when the Son of man is revealed.

After diligently studying the previous verses on the second coming of Christ, it is plainly written that the appearing of Christ from heaven, the resurrection of the dead, and the day of the Lord all occur on the same day. There can absolutely be no seven year gap between these events as we have been lead to believe by the pre-tribulation doctrine. Any serious student of the Bible should be able to ascertain that the seven year gap theory clearly is not a biblical teaching. I urge you to get your revelation not to follow another man's. I believe that because of misinterpretation of scripture many are going to be rudely surprised. Even today it is being preached that Jesus is returning December 12th 2012. I believe according to scripture this is false but at the same time no one knows the time Jesus will return. There are just signs that must align first.

THE RAPTURE: DETAILS OF THE SECOND COMING OF CHRIST

The Shaky Ground

We have already examined one of the foremost deviations from the truth that is a foundational stone of the pre-tribulation doctrine, the doctrine of imminence. So we will now examine, in light of the Scriptures, some of the other doctrines of this shaky ground the pre-tribulation rapture belief is based on.

The pre-tribulation view of the rapture is supported by the belief that in 2 Thessalonians 2 is the Holy Spirit. And since the Holy Spirit indwells all believers, the believers must be raptured before the Anti-Christ is revealed. The Scriptures state it this way concerning the question,

2 Thessalonians 2:6-9 And now ye know what withholdeth that he might be revealed in his time. For the mystery of iniquity doth already work: only he who now letteth *will let,* until he be taken out of the way. And then shall that Wicked be revealed, whom the Lord shall consume with the spirit of his mouth, and shall destroy with the brightness of his coming: *Even him,* whose coming is after the working of Satan with all power and signs and lying wonders,

There are those who preach that the Holy Spirit will restrain the saints but my question is to produce some biblical evidence of this belief? How many Scriptures are there to support this view? Not a single one, as any pre-tribulation teacher will tell you. They admit that their belief is simply an assumption on their part and is the most logical conclusion to be drawn from the Scriptures. No precept upon precept, line upon line here, just assumption and logical reasoning. And what does the Bible say about logical reasoning?

2 Corinthians 10:5 Casting down imaginations, and every high thing that exalteth itself against the knowledge of God, and bringing into captivity every thought to the obedience of Christ;

The Restrainer Must Be Removed

2 Thessalonians 2:6-12 And now ye know what withholdeth that he might be revealed in his time. For the mystery of iniquity doth already work: only he who now letteth *will let,* until he be taken out of the way. And then shall that Wicked be revealed, whom the Lord shall consume with the spirit of his mouth, and shall destroy with the brightness of his coming: *Even him,* whose coming is after the working of Satan with all power and signs and lying wonders, And with all deceivableness of unrighteousness in them that perish; because they received not the love of the truth, that they might be saved. And for this cause God shall send them strong delusion, that they should believe a lie: That they all might be damned who believed not the truth, but had pleasure in unrighteousness.

Wiersbe's Expository Outlines on the New Testament Satan's mystery of iniquity is already working in the world, and we can see its godless activities increasing rapidly. What, then, holds back Satan's evil program and the rise of the Antichrist? God has a "restrainer" in the world, **which we believe** is the Holy Spirit working in and through the Church. God has "times and seasons" marked out, and even Satan cannot get God off schedule.

THE RAPTURE: DETAILS OF THE SECOND COMING OF CHRIST

1 Thessalonions 5:1 But of the times and the seasons, brethren, ye have no need that I write unto you.

The One who hinders is the Spirit, and He will continue to hinder Satan's activities until He is taken out of the midst when the Church is raptured. Of course, the Spirit will still work on earth, since people will believe and be saved after The Rapture: but His hindering ministry through the body of Christ will end. This will give Satan free course to fill the cup of iniquity to the full.

THE NEW SCOFIELD STUDY BIBLE – KJV 2 THESSALONIANS 2:3 The order of events is:

(1) The working of the mystery of lawlessness under divine restraint which had already begun in the apostle's time and which has been expanding throughout the Church Age.

(2) The removal of that which restrains the mystery of lawlessness. There are various views as to the identity of the restraining influence. The use of the male pronoun "he" indicates that it is a person. It seems evident that it is the Holy Spirit:

(a) in the Old Testament the Holy Spirit acts as a restrainer of iniquity (Genesis 6:3);

(b) the restrainer is referred to by the use of both neuter and male genders as in John 14:16-17; 16:12-13 concerning the coming of the Holy Spirit; and

(c) it will be when the restrainer is taken out, concerning the coming of the Holy Spirit; and

(d) it will be when the restrainer is "taken out of the way" that the man of sin will be revealed; this will be when the Church is translated and the Spirit's restraining ministry through it will cease. Observe, however, that it is not said that the restrainer will be "taken away," but "taken out of the way"; thus the Holy Spirit will continue a divine activity to the end-time, though not as a restrainer of evil through the Church.

THE RAPTURE: DETAILS OF THE SECOND COMING OF CHRIST

Study the Bible

2 Thessalonians 2:6, 7 And now ye know what withholdeth that he might be revealed in his time. For the mystery of iniquity doth already work: only he who now letteth *will let,* until he be taken out of the way.

The One who is "restraining" is probably a reference to the Holy Spirit in His restraining ministry through the Church. "Restraining" emphasizes what is presently a strong effort by the Holy Spirit to hold back the maximal exhibition of evil and the advent of the Antichrist. In the present age the Spirit is operative in restraining evil. During the Tribulation, the Holy Spirit's ministry of restraining will be moved out of the way, probably as a result of the rapture of the Church. This is not a departure of the Holy Spirit, for He is omnipresent, but rather it is a temporary end of one of His gracious ministries. A "mystery" is a secret which God has revealed, one which lies beyond human knowledge. The verse teaches us that this evil is already active, though at the present its manifestation is hidden from us. In the above mentioned sources of the pre-tribulation doctrine, not one claims to have biblical evidence for the Holy Spirit being the restrainer. They base their belief on assumptions and probabilities.

Bible doctrine cannot be based on what we think or assume, but must be established precept upon precept and line upon line. One well known faith teacher who has written a book on the rapture has said publicly that he told the Lord that he did not have one verse of Scripture for one of the revelations He had given for his doctrine He then stated that Jesus told him; "just trust me on this one." We cannot take someone's word for doctrine. Scripture has to be our guide. I have heard teaching that also states that God commissioned the 144,000 who are sealed to preach the gospel during the great tribulation, although the Bible says absolutely nothing about the role of the 144,000 as evangelists. This theory is based solely and entirely on the assumption of men, and is not taught in the Scriptures! How arrogant to even think that Jesus would give you understanding of a doctrine and tell you to teach it to His people, and not provide a scriptural basis for it. What does the Bible say about the restrainer? And is there any biblical support for who he is? The Bible does speak of one, who will cease to restrain the evil one, and when he ceases to restrain, the Bible does speak of one who will cease to restrain the evil one, and when he ceases to restrain, the man of sin will be revealed.

Daniel 12:1 And at that time shall Michael stand up, the great prince which standeth for the children of thy people: and there shall be a time of trouble, such as never was since there was a nation *even* to that same time: and at that time thy people shall be delivered, every one that shall be found written in the book.

The fact that Michael will standeth is an indication that he will stand still, or cease to restrain. Up until this time Michael has been standeth for warring on the behalf of the nation of Israel, but now he stands still, or ceases to fight for Israel. It should also be noted in Daniel 12:1 that when Michael stands up, the time of trouble the great tribulation begins. This is exactly in line with 2 Thessalonians 2:7-8 that speaks of the restrainer being taken out of the way, the anti-Christ being revealed, and the beginning of the great tribulation. We can see Michael's role as the restrainer in more detail.

THE RAPTURE: DETAILS OF THE SECOND COMING OF CHRIST

Revelations 12:7-17 And there was war in heaven: Michael and his angels fought against the dragon; and the dragon fought and his angels, And prevailed not; neither was their place found any more in heaven. And the great dragon was cast out, that old serpent, called the Devil, and Satan, which deceiveth the whole world: he was cast out into the earth, and his angels were cast out with him. And I heard a loud voice saying in heaven, Now is come salvation, and strength, and the kingdom of our God, and the power of his Christ: for the accuser of our brethren is cast down, which accused them before our God day and night. And they overcame him by the blood of the Lamb, and by the word of their testimony; and they loved not their lives unto the death. Therefore rejoice, *ye* heavens, and ye that dwell in them. Woe to the inhabiters of the earth and of the sea! for the devil is come down unto you, having great wrath, because he knoweth that he hath but a short time. And when the dragon saw that he was cast unto the earth, he persecuted the woman which brought forth the man *child.* And to the woman were given two wings of a great eagle, that she might fly into the wilderness, into her place, where she is nourished for a time, and times, and half a time, from the face of the serpent. And the serpent cast out of his mouth water as a flood after the woman, that he might cause her to be carried away of the flood. And the earth helped the woman, and the earth opened her mouth, and swallowed up the flood which the dragon cast out of his mouth. And the dragon was wroth with the woman, and went to make war with the remnant of her seed, which keep the commandments of God, and have the testimony of Jesus Christ.

Those which keep the commandments of God, and have the testimony of Jesus Christ are believers in Christ, Jew and Gentile alike. These are the ones the fury of the devil will be unleashed upon during the great tribulation.

Satan's Wrath

Reveenings 12:12-14 Therefore rejoice, *ye* heavens, and ye that dwell in them. Woe to the inhabiters of the earth and of the sea! for the devil is come down unto you, having great wrath, because he knoweth that he hath but a short time. And when the dragon saw that he was cast unto the earth, he persecuted the woman which brought forth the man *child*. And to the woman were given two wings of a great eagle, that she might fly into the wilderness, into her place, where she is nourished for a time, and times, and half a time, from the face of the serpent.

It clearly shows that the devil will have a time when he will unleash his wrath upon Jews and Christians alike. The time frame for the venting of his wrath is very clearly shown to be three and one-half years. These Scriptures reveal to us that the time of the Great Tribulation is the devil's wrath, not God's. One of the major errors of the pre-tribulation doctrine is the belief that the Great Tribulation is the wrath of God, which it clearly is not. The fact that there is not one single Scripture to support the view of the departure of the Church as the restraining force against the revealing of the anti-Christ, should cause any serious Bible study to re-examine this issue.

Pre-Tribulation Arguments

1. The Great Tribulation is the wrath of God and lasts for seven years. We are not appointed unto wrath.

This is perhaps one of the biggest stumbling blocks of the pre-tribulation doctrine. To believe that the Great Tribulation is the wrath of God, and that it lasts for a period of seven years, is a false belief and closes the door to any further revelation from the Holy Spirit on the doctrine of the rapture. Jesus very clearly taught in Matthew 24 that the great tribulation begins when the abomination of desolation is set up, which according to Daniel the prophet occurs in the middle of the week, not at the beginning.

2. The Holy Spirit is the restrainer.

This foundational stone of the pre-tribulation doctrine has absolutely no scriptural basis, as admitted by those who teach it. To believe that the Church must be removed before the anti-Christ is revealed is in direct opposition to the Scriptures.

2 Thessalonians 2:1-3 Now we beseech you, brethren, by the coming of our Lord Jesus Christ, and *by* our gathering together unto him, That ye be not soon shaken in mind, or be troubled, neither by spirit, nor by word, nor by letter as from us, as that the day of Christ is at hand. Let no man deceive you by any means: for *that day shall not come,* except there come a falling away first, and that man of sin be revealed, the son of perdition;

3. The Church is not mentioned after Revelations Chapter 4.

The fact that the Church is not mentioned after John was told to "come up hither" is believed to portray the fact that the Church had been raptured at that time. Any earnest study of the Bible would see that the message to John to "come up hither" has nothing to do with the rapture. While the Church specifically is not mentioned after Revelations Chapter 4, there are several references to saints who are present during the Great Tribulation. To believe that this command to John is a reference to the rapture is a real stretch of the imagination,

THE RAPTURE: DETAILS OF THE SECOND COMING OF CHRIST

to say nothing of the injustice it does to Scripture. Any pre-tribulation teacher would readily admit that the Church is made up of "saints." But when it comes to teaching eschatology, they seem to have a lapse in memory, forgetting that the word saints is mentioned numerous times in the epistles in reference to the Church.

4. The doctrine of imminence.

The belief that Jesus could come at any moment without any signs or without any Bible prophecies yet to be fulfilled is to deny the Scriptures.

Acts 3:20, 21 And he shall send Jesus Christ, which before was preached unto you: Whom the heaven must receive until the times of restitution of all things, which God hath spoken by the mouth of all his holy prophets since the world began.

One of the head components of the pre-tribulation doctrine mentioned that Israel had to be in their homeland before the coming of Christ. Here is what he says in his own words; "The events leading up to the coming of the Messiah Jesus are sprinkled throughout the Old and New Testament prophets like pieces of a puzzle. The key piece of the puzzle which was missing until our time was that Israel had to be back in their ancient homeland, re-established as a nation.

If Israel had to be back in their ancient homeland and re-established as a nation, isn't that enough to convince anyone that Jesus could not possibly have come before 1948, when Israel was indeed re-established as a nation?

5. The coming of the Lord Jesus Christ and the rapture of the saints are two separate events, separated by at least seven years. Not only are they separate events, but the rapture occurs before the coming.

The apostle Paul makes it very clear that the coming and the rapture are a connected event. The rapture is preceded by His coming according to scripture.

2 Thessalonians 2:1 Now we beseech you, brethren, by the coming of our Lord Jesus Christ, and *by* our gathering together unto him,

While the pre-tribulation teachers reverse the order of events concerning the coming of Christ and the gathering together, Paul makes it very clear that Christ's coming precedes the gathering together. In order to make the pre-tribulation doctrine work, one would have to reverse the order that the Holy Spirit taught through the apostle Paul. Paul places the coming before the gathering together. We must not take such liberty with the Word that we so blatantly misquote the Word in order to prove our doctrine.

6. The 144,000 Jews who are sealed preach the gospel {evangelize} during the great tribulation.

This is one of the most irresponsible teachings of the pre-tribulation rapture. The Bible says absolutely nothing about the 144,000 being evangelists, and no where indicates they evangelize during the great tribulation. The only thing the Bible tells about them is the fact that they are sealed and protected from the wrath of God which is ready to be poured out on the unrepentant sinners of the world. To conjure up something that clearly is not in the Scriptures in order to prove or establish doctrine is totally unacceptable in studying to show ourselves approved unto God? Nearly every pre-tribulation teacher teaches that the 144,000 Jews who are sealed prior to the wrath of God being poured out, are evangelists who preach during the great tribulation. The wrath of God being poured out, are evangelists who preach during the great tribulation. Although there is not one single verse of Scripture to support this theory, this is one of the ludicrous errors so readily espoused by almost all pre-tribulation teachers. Please check out the Bible references concerning the 144,000 for yourself, and see if anything is mentioned about them being evangelists. If you can see that this is purely an assumption on the part of pre-tribulation teachers, perhaps you would be led to check out their other theories as well. If it is not precept upon precept and line upon line, it should be thrown out!

Escaping Before the Great Tribulation?

In the following Scriptures you will find a scenario similar to the teaching of the pre-tribulation rapture today. Jeremiah had prophesied according to God's instruction that Israel was to go into captivity for a period of seventy years. Hananiah however, who was a people-pleaser, prophesied that all of Israel and the vessels of the Lord's house that had been taken into captivity thus far would be brought back before the seventy years expired. He prophesied that the captivity would be over within two years of his prophecy. This can be likened to the "prophets" today who are teaching the pre-tribulation rapture, declaring that Israel (the Church) will not go into captivity (the great tribulation). Please read carefully the text of Ezekiel 13 and Jeremiah 28 below, and see how God dealt with the prophets who taught rebellion against the Lord and caused God's people to trust in a lie. Some teachers of the pre-tribulation doctrine, when asked what they would do if they found that the Church was present during the Great Tribulation, and Jesus had not yet come, responded that they would simply admit they were wrong, and no one would be injured. The truth is however, that false teaching concerning the coming of the Lord can overthrow the faith of the saints. For this reason, it is imperative that ministers of the gospel unite and come into unity concerning this doctrine. We must not continue to bring confusion to the body of Christ by teaching conflicting views of the coming of the Lord and our gathering together unto him. Our attitude must be one of love for each other and for the truth of God's holy word. Our love for truth must outweigh our desire to be right in our own eyes,

THE RAPTURE: DETAILS OF THE SECOND COMING OF CHRIST

and we must consider that as teachers we will incur the stricter judgment concerning doctrine.

Ezekiel 13:1-16 And the word of the LORD came unto me, saying, Son of man, prophesy against the prophets of Israel that prophesy, and say thou unto them that prophesy out of their own hearts, Hear ye the word of the LORD; Thus saith the Lord GOD; Woe unto the foolish prophets, that follow their own spirit, and have seen nothing! O Israel, thy prophets are like the foxes in the deserts. Ye have not gone up into the gaps, neither made up the hedge for the house of Israel to stand in the battle in the day of the LORD. They have seen vanity and lying divination, saying, The LORD saith: and the LORD hath not sent them: and they have made *others* to hope that they would confirm the word. Have ye not seen a vain vision, and have ye not spoken a lying divination, whereas ye say, The LORD saith *it;* albeit I have not spoken? Therefore thus saith the Lord GOD; Because ye have spoken vanity, and seen lies, therefore, behold, I *am* against you, saith the Lord GOD. And mine hand shall be upon the prophets that see vanity, and that divine lies: they shall not be in the assembly of my people, neither shall they be written in the writing of the house of Israel, neither shall they enter into the land of Israel; and ye shall know that I *am* the Lord GOD. Because, even because they have seduced my people, saying, Peace; and *there was* no peace; and one built up a wall, and, lo, others daubed it with untempered *morter:* Say unto them which daub *it* with untempered *morter,* that it shall fall: there shall be an overflowing shower; and ye, O great hailstones, shall fall; and a stormy wind shall rend *it.* Lo, when the wall is fallen, shall it not be said unto you, Where *is* the daubing wherewith ye have daubed *it?* Therefore thus saith the Lord GOD; I will even rend *it* with a stormy wind in my fury; and there shall be an overflowing shower in mine anger, and great hailstones in *my* fury to consume *it.* So will I break down the wall that ye have daubed with untempered *morter,* and bring it down to the ground, so that the foundation thereof shall be discovered, and it shall fall, and ye shall be consumed in the midst thereof: and ye shall know that I *am* the LORD. Thus will I accomplish my wrath upon the wall, and upon them that have daubed it with untempered *morter,* and will say unto you, The wall *is* no *more,* neither they that daubed it; *To wit,* the prophets of Israel which prophesy concerning Jerusalem, and which see visions of peace for her, and *there is* no peace, saith the Lord GOD.

Jeremiah 28:17 And it came to pass the same year, in the beginning of the reign of Zedekiah king of Judah, in the fourth year, *and* in the fifth month, *that* Hananiah the son of Azur the prophet, which *was* of Gibeon, spake unto me in the house of the LORD, in the presence of the priests and of all the people, saying, Thus speaketh the LORD of hosts, the God of Israel, saying, I have broken the yoke of the king of Babylon. Within two full years will I bring again into this place all the vessels of the LORD'S house, that Nebuchadnezzar king of Babylon took away from this place, and carried them to Babylon: And I will bring again to this place Jeconiah the son of Jehoiakim king of Judah, with all the captives of Judah, that went into Babylon, saith the LORD: for I will break the yoke of the king of Babylon. Then the prophet Jeremiah said unto the prophet Hananiah in the presence of the priests, and in the presence of all the people that stood in the house of the LORD, Even the prophet Jeremiah said, Amen: the LORD do so: the LORD perform thy words which thou hast prophesied, to bring again the vessels of the LORD'S house, and all that is carried away captive, from Babylon into this place. Nevertheless hear thou now this word that I speak in thine ears, and in the ears of all the people; The prophets that have been before me and before thee of old prophesied both against many countries, and against great kingdoms, of war, and of evil, and of pestilence. The prophet which prophesieth of peace, when the word of the prophet shall come to pass, *then* shall the prophet be known, that the LORD hath truly sent him. Then Hananiah the prophet took the yoke from off the prophet Jeremiah's neck, and brake it. And Hananiah spake in the presence of all the people, saying, Thus saith the LORD; Even so will I break the yoke of Nebuchadnezzar king of Babylon from the neck of all nations within the space of two full years. And the prophet Jeremiah went his way. Then the word of the LORD came unto Jeremiah *the prophet,* after that Hananiah the prophet had broken the yoke from off the neck of the prophet Jeremiah, saying, Go and tell Hananiah, saying, Thus saith the LORD; Thou hast broken the yokes of wood; but thou shalt make for them yokes of iron. For thus saith the LORD of hosts, the God of Israel; I have put a yoke of iron upon the neck of all these nations, that they may serve Nebuchadnezzar king of Babylon; and they shall serve him: and I have given him the beasts of the field also. Then said the prophet Jeremiah unto Hananiah the prophet, Hear now, Hananiah; The LORD hath not sent thee; but thou makest this people to trust in a lie. Therefore thus saith the LORD; Behold, I will cast thee from off the face of the earth: this year thou shalt die, because thou hast taught rebellion against the LORD. So Hananiah the prophet died the same year in the seventh month.

It may very well be that the Lord will bring swift judgment on those who cause His people to trust in a lie and teach rebellion against the Lord by prophesying saying the Lord told me, the pre-tribulation rapture. Many teachers claim they are not prophesying but are only teaching the pre-tribulation rapture, but almost all of them are saying in their writings and teachings; God told me which is equivalent of prophesying. What are the effects of false doctrine? What is the result of teaching erroneous doctrine? Can the doctrine of pre-tribulations cause any real harm? Most certainly it can! Listen to what Paul has to say about the effects of false doctrine on those who receive it.

2 Timothy 2:16-18 But shun profane *and* vain babblings: for they will increase unto more ungodliness. And their word will eat as doth a canker: of whom is Hymenaeus and Philetus; Who concerning the truth have erred, saying that the resurrection is past already; and overthrow the faith of some.

What will be the result of teaching and receiving the false teaching of the pre-tribulation rapture? The Bible says that it can overthrow our faith. What will the saints who believe in the pre-tribulation rapture do when they realize they are in the Great Tribulation period, and that they have been lied to concerning the rapture? I cannot say for certain how they will respond, but I would not want to be in the same category as Hymenaeus and Philetus who were teaching the false doctrine that caused others to stray from the truth. It seems that God is remaining somewhat silent at this time, but it may be that when the Church has indeed entered into the great tribulation, that the Lord may judge quickly and severely those who continue to teach this false doctrine.

The Anti-Christ

The Bible tells us that the anti-Christ will have dominion over the whole earth when he comes into power, and that no one will be able to buy or sell unless they receive his mark or the number of his name. This man will seem to be the savior to our world.

Revelations 13:16, 17 And he causeth all, both small and great, rich and poor, free and bond, to receive a mark in their right hand, or in their foreheads: And that no man might buy or sell, save he that had the mark, or the name of the beast, or the number of his name.

The technology is already in place to imbed micro-chips beneath the skin of humans in order to identify them and to track their activities. This is exactly what the anti-Christ will do when he assumes power. There are more and more things being created to know where we are at all times. It is appearing to be a help but it will not be a help when the Anti-Christ takes over. The Bible tells us that whoever receives the mark of the beast will spend eternity in the lake of fire that burns with fire and brimstone, that was prepared for the devil and his angels Incredibly, some are teaching and deceiving Christians into thinking that they can receive the mark of the beast in order to conduct business, and later repent and be restored to eternal life.

Everyone who receives the mark of the beast or the number of his name will spend eternity in the lake of fire!

Revelatios 14:9-11 And the third angel followed them, saying with a loud voice, If any man worship the beast and his image, and receive *his* mark in his forehead, or in his hand, The same shall drink of the wine of the wrath of God, which is poured out without mixture into the cup of his indignation; and he shall be tormented with fire and brimstone in the presence of the holy angels, and in the presence of the Lamb: And the smoke of their torment ascendeth up for ever and ever: and they have no rest day nor night, who worship the beast and his image, and whosoever receiveth the mark of his name.

Everyone who receives the mark of the beast or the number of his name will spend eternity with him in the lake of fire that burns with fire and brimstone. Let no one deceive you with teachings that speak contrary to the word. Anyone who teaches salvation after receiving the mark of the beast or the number of his name is terribly deceived, and is setting up those that hear this false doctrine to fall into the hands of the devil.

What about the events of September 11, 2001, when terrorists struck at the heart of America by attacking the World Trade Center and the Pentagon? In an effort to prevent future terrorist activity, many Americans are willing to give up all their Constitutional rights, in order to feel they will be protected from terrorist attacks. And it appears that our government officials are very willing to take them from us. The truth is that we do not have to blindly give up our rights as American citizens in order to live safely in our own country. Certain people who are in power over the nations of the world have long awaited an opportunity like this to bring the entire world to its knees. Already, American citizens are being asked to give up their rights as sovereign nationals, under the pretense of national security. I am all in favor of national security, but I am convinced that we do not need to bring all American citizens under the bondage and complete rule of the

Government in order to obtain that security. America, as a sovereign nation was established under the principles of being a free people. Many offered their lives in defense of that freedom. We should never, under any circumstances give up that freedom that so many have fought and died for. It has already become legal to listen to phone conversations without a search warrant.

It is my personal belief that we are being conditioned to receive the mark of the beast even now, through the recent events that have rocked our nation. I am also of the opinion that we must not bow to the anti-Christ system and cooperate willingly to bring ourselves into bondage to that system. You can bet that the anti-Christ spirit is at work through the disasters we suffered at the hands of ungodly cowards through the attacks on our nation. Just as millions of American citizens are required to waive their Constitutional rights today, the mark of the Beast will also be voluntary. The Bible tells us that we will be given a choice when it is offered to us. We are being offered choices today by our very own Government and corporate entities. When the mark is offered, every person in the world will need it in order to work, and to buy and sell. That will be the point, you won't be able to buy food and the necessities of life without it. Since we are being led into it a little at a time, the decision won't be too hard for most people to make in that day. Of course, we have to feed our families, don't we? If we are willing to give up our rights now, it won't be hard at all to do in that day. And who could blame you, you do have to provide for your family, don't you? Just remember, it will cost you everything in that day. By receiving the mark, an eternal sentence will be issued against those who take it;

eternity, in the lake of fire that was prepared for the devil and his angels!

The Church itself has unknowingly submitted to the rule of the Federal and State governments. The Government is not yet exercising all its authority over the Church, but you can bet that they will as the reign of the anti-Christ governmental system grows nearer. Please research this information for yourself, and see what you find.

There is a plan already in place to create a one-world super power that will enable the anti-Christ to rule the entire world. That document is named: US

Leaders of many nations, including the US, are hard at work to devise a peace proposal that can be agreed upon by Israel. Numerous diplomatic meetings have been held and will continue until there is a seven-year covenant of peace. Of course, this will be a false peace, and will signal the last seven years of history as we know it. The Declaration of Principles can be viewed from various Internet sites. Israel is on a collision course with the ungodly nations of the world that seek her demise. There will be a man who rises to prominence internationally, who will step in and supposedly bring world peace. The Bible calls him the Beast and the Anti-Christ. At that time, a seven-year agreement will be signed with Israel and others that will signal the beginning of the seventieth week of Daniel. When that occurs, all that has been prophesied about the last days will transpire, and conclude with the return of Jesus Christ as the Lion of the tribe of Judah who raptures His Church, and pours out His unbridled wrath upon the ungodly people of the world. After His wrath is finished, He will rule the nations with a rod of iron. Then, and only then will the nations of the earth enjoy true peace. Jesus will rule with His saints for a period of one thousand years, and the earth will be at rest. We are living in the very days that the earth and every living thing is groaning in anticipation of the coming of the restoration and renewal of the earth, and the redemption of His saints. What a glorious day that will be!

Until that time, we must be busy about the Father's business in the earth, preaching the gospel of the kingdom, and doing His work. He said that we would do the same works that He did. Surely today is the day to believe all that He has said in His Word, and to do the works He said we should do. The Bible says that Jesus is coming for a glorious Church, one without spot or blemish. He is sanctifying and preparing us to be that glorious Bride that longs for His coming. We must come together in these days as His one glorious Body, triumphant in the earth. The Church Jesus is coming for will be victorious over sin and the cares of the world. We shall all soon see Him coming from the heavens with power and Greater Glory. Our work as flesh and blood beings will be finished, our troubles in this life will be over, and we will be clothed upon with immortality. Prior to that time the Church of Jesus Christ will shine in the brightness of His glory, and will be thoroughly transformed into His likeness. The last of those who are to be saved will come in at that time, all Israel will be saved, and the earth will be at rest under the rule of Christ.

Saved After Death?

Can A Person Be Saved After Their Death?

Some believe that God's love is so powerful and overwhelming, that it will eventually melt the hearts of every single person, thus no one will ever end up in hell for all of eternity. This is completely false. God does love us but after death it is too late.

As you will see in the specific Scripture verses I will give you in this article, God is making it very clear and very plain that we have to accept His free gift of eternal salvation through His Son Jesus this side of heaven, not the next. In other words, we only have this one earthly lifetime to find and accept Jesus, and we have to do it before we die and leave this world. If we think we can do it after we die and cross over, we will find out very quickly that we were sadly mistaken and will thus have to pay with our eternal lives in the most horrible place imaginable.

It will get them to put off making this life-altering decision until either later in their life or when they die and cross over. They will see no need or have any desire to want to repent since their sins will be forgiven anyway once they die and meet Jesus face-to-face for their eternal salvation. As a result, many people are going to be led straight into the pits of hell once they die and cross over as a result of putting off accepting Jesus as their personal Lord and Savior in this one earthly lifetime in which they had to do it in.

How some of these Christian pastors are falling for this demonic doctrine of Univeralsim is simply beyond me, as it goes directly against what God is telling us in His written Word on how He has the big picture set up with all of us.

Now I will go to the specific Scripture verses which will answer this question once and for all since these verses are all coming direct from the mouth of the Lord Himself.

Once again, I believe God is meaning exactly what He is saying in each one of these verses, and I thus see no room for any type of Universalistic doctrine in any of these verses.

1. It is Appointed for Men to Die Once – And Then We Face Judgment

This first verse, in my opinion, completely answers this question as to whether or not we can still get saved after our death and departure from this world. Here is the verse, and then I will point out a few key things to really grab a hold of.

Hebrews 9:27 And as it is appointed unto men once to die, but after this the judgment:

Notice the following:

a) If God ever had any opening in one of His verses to let all of us know that we could still receive eternal salvation through His Son Jesus after we had already died and crossed over, this verse would be it. If this was a possibility with the Lord, then I believe He would have put that kind of statement in this verse. But notice He did not.

This verse is flat out telling us that we will only get one earthly lifetime to get our act together with Him. We are not going to be reincarnated back into another body to get several more chances to find and accept Jesus this side of heaven. We only have one earthly lifetime in which to be able to do this.

b) And then notice what it says after our one earthly lifetime is up down here – we will then all face judgment with God Almighty Himself. There is no wording whatsoever that we will get some kind of extra time on the other side to find and accept Jesus.

This verse is telling us that we are going to face judgment – and this judgment is going to be based on what we have done down here on this earth. There is nothing in this verse that will tell us that we will be judged on anything we will be doing on the other side once we die and cross over into it.

If God ever had one verse with a big huge opening in it where He could tell us that we could get saved after our deaths, this verse would be it. There is an opening in this verse wide enough and big enough to drive a Mack truck through. But notice how short, sweet and very straight-forward and direct-to-the-point this verse is.

Bottom line – we only have this one life down here on this earth to live, and after this one life has been lived, we will then die and cross over to face God for our own personal judgments on our lives. And again, this judgment is based upon what we have done down here on this earth, not for what might have occurred on the other side once we have died and crossed over.

The fact that God is completely leaving out any kind of possibility that we could get saved on the other side of heaven is flat out telling me this is not even a possibility with Him. We thus have to take this very serious verse at face value and believe what it is directly telling us. We cannot try and take this verse out, or try to discount it because it does not agree with how we think God should have the big picture all set up.

2. God Will Judge Us for the Works That Were Done in the Body

These next verses are now going to add more to the first verse above. These verses are specifically talking about all saved and born-again Christians. The first verse will completely set the stage for all of us.

This first verse is telling us that we will all have to appear before the Judgment Seat of Jesus, and from there, we will be judged for the things we have done in the body. The 4 keys words to really sharpen in on are things that we have "done in the body."

I believe the word "body" is referring to our earthly, human, physical bodies. As a result, we will all be judged for the things we have done down here on this earth, not for what might have occurred on the other side once we had died and crossed over. And again, if there was any kind of possibility that we would also be judged for things that might have occurred on the other side once we had died and crossed over, then Jesus would have specifically told us so in this verse.

But when Jesus is specifically isolating all of the things we have done in our earthly physical bodies as to what will be judged, then you know He is talking about what we have done down here on this earth. This thus leaves no room or any kind of possibility that we can get saved on the other side of heaven.

Here are four more good verses to add into this argument:

2 Corinthians 5:10 For we must all appear before the judgment seat of Christ; that every one may receive the things *done* in *his* body, according to that he hath done, whether *it be* good or bad.

1 Corinthians 3:8 Now he that planteth and he that watereth are one: and every man shall receive his own reward according to his own labour.

Revelations 22:12 And, behold, I come quickly; and my reward *is* with me, to give every man according as his work shall be.

Revelations 2:23 And I will kill her children with death; and all the churches shall know that I am he which searcheth the reins and hearts: and I will give unto every one of you according to your works.

We are going to be rewarded by Jesus for the labor and works we have done for Him down here on this earth. And again, these are for works and labors that are done down here on this earth, not for they might have occurred up in heaven once we had entered there.

Again, if there was any possibility that we could get saved up in heaven, then Jesus would have put that kind of specific wording in all of these verses.

3. The Great White Throne Judgment

If all Christians will come before the Judgment Seat of Jesus for their own personal judgments in Him, then what kind of judgment will all of the unsaved have to face before the Lord?

This next verse will answer this question for you, and this judgment is called the Great White Throne Judgment. Here is the verse, and then I will point a few key things in this verse to really grab a hold of:

Revelations 20:11-14 And I saw a great white throne, and him that sat on it, from whose face the earth and the heaven fled away; and there was found no place for them. And I saw the dead, small and great, stand before God; and the books were opened: and another book was opened, which is *the book* of life: and the dead were judged out of those things which were written in the books, according to their works. And the sea gave up the dead which were in it; and death and hell delivered up the dead which were in them: and they were judged every man according to their works. And death and hell were cast into the lake of fire. This is the second death.

Notice several key things in this verse:

a) This judgment is only for the unsaved, it is not for all born-again Christians. How do you know this? Because this passage is using the words that the "dead" are the ones who are appearing before the Lord for this final judgment.

Also note the wording that "Death and Hades delivered up the dead who were in them." This phrase is telling you that all of the people who are appearing before the Lord in this last and final judgment are all coming from Hades, which is where they have all been during the 1000 year millennial reign of Jesus.

Born-again Christians are not dead, we are all fully alive, especially since we have now all died and entered into heaven, and then came back down with Jesus to rule with Him during the 1000 year Millennium Kingdom.

And then notice what the dead are being judged for? They are being "judged according to their works." And again, these are works that were done down here on this earth, not for what might have occurred on the other side once they had died and crossed over.

b) Again, if there was any possibility that the unsaved could get saved once they die and cross over, this verse would definitely be telling us this. But once again, it does not. As such, we cannot attempt to add something to this verse that is not in there.

This verse, along with the verses above about Jesus rewarding and judging us for what we have all done in the body, are all showing us that both of these judgments will be made on what we have done down here on this earth, not for they might have occurred on the other side once we had died and crossed over.

How any Christian can fall for the doctrine of Universalism, when these kinds of verses from Scripture are all so clear and plain is just beyond me. If you believe that all of the Holy Bible is truly the inspired and infallible Word of our Holy God, then there is simply no other conclusion you can come to on this topic.

4. The Rich Man and Lazarus

The last verse I will leave you with that will also answer this question is the one on Lazarus and the rich man. After they had both died, Lazarus goes straight to Abraham's bosom, and the rich man ends up going straight down into hell for the kind of life he had lived.

And then notice what happens next. The rich man is crying out that he is burning alive in a flame of fire. And then Abraham answers the rich man telling him that it is now too late. There is a great gulf separating these two places from one another and the rich man cannot cross over into Abraham's bosom where Lazarus is now at.

Also notice the rich man says absolutely nothing about being able to make it right with the Lord after he had died and entered into hell. The implication is all there that this rich man immediately entered into hell right after his death. This verse is thus confirming the first verse listed above that we are appointed to die once, and then when we die, judgment is then set on our lives as to where we will end up going.

Again, this is another verse where there is a huge opening for the Lord to tell us that we can get saved after we die. But once again, there is absolutely no wording whatsoever in this verse that we can do this with the Lord. This verse is following the same pattern as the rest of the above verses are doing, all showing us that we have to find and accept Jesus in this one earthly lifetime.

Here is this verse, once more driving home the point that we have to get saved this side of heaven, not the next side:

"There was a certain rich man who was clothed in purple and fine linen and fared sumptuously every day. But there was a certain beggar named Lazarus, full of sores, who was laid at his gate, desiring to be fed with the crumbs which fell from the rich man's table. Moreover the dogs came and licked his sores. So it was the beggar died, and was carried by the angels to Abraham's bosom. The rich man also died and was buried.

And being in torments in Hades (Hell), he lifted up his eyes and saw Abraham afar off, and Lazarus in his bosom. Then he cried and said, "Father Abraham, have mercy on me, and send Lazarus that he may dip the tip of his finger in water and cool my tongue; for I am tormented in this flame. But Abraham said, Son, remember that in your lifetime you received your good things, and likewise Lazarus evil things; but now he is comforted and you are tormented. And besides all this, between us and you there is a great gulf fixed, so that those who want to pass from here to you cannot, nor can those from there pass to us.

THE RAPTURE: DETAILS OF THE SECOND COMING OF CHRIST

Luke 16:19-31 There was a certain rich man, which was clothed in purple and fine linen, and fared sumptuously every day: And there was a certain beggar named Lazarus, which was laid at his gate, full of sores, And desiring to be fed with the crumbs which fell from the rich man's table: moreover the dogs came and licked his sores. And it came to pass, that the beggar died, and was carried by the angels into Abraham's bosom: the rich man also died, and was buried; And in hell he lift up his eyes, being in torments, and seeth Abraham afar off, and Lazarus in his bosom. And he cried and said, Father Abraham, have mercy on me, and send Lazarus, that he may dip the tip of his finger in water, and cool my tongue; for I am tormented in this flame. But Abraham said, Son, remember that thou in thy lifetime receivedst thy good things, and likewise Lazarus evil things: but now he is comforted, and thou art tormented. And beside all this, between us and you there is a great gulf fixed: so that they which would pass from hence to you cannot; neither can they pass to us, that *would come* from thence. Then he said, I pray thee therefore, father, that thou wouldest send him to my father's house: For I have five brethren; that he may testify unto them, lest they also come into this place of torment. Abraham saith unto him, They have Moses and the prophets; let them hear them. And he said, Nay, father Abraham: but if one went unto them from the dead, they will repent. And he said unto him, If they hear not Moses and the prophets, neither will they be persuaded, though one rose from the dead.

Conclusion

If there was any kind of possibility that we could get saved after our death and departure from this world, then I believe God would be telling us so in these kinds of verses. But since

He is not, we have to take Him at His Word and believe what these verses are literally telling us.

This is the way our God has the big picture all set up and woe to any man or woman who will try and take this doctrine out of our basic tenets and try to replace it with the false doctrine of Universalism. With all of us only having one short lifetime in which to find and accept Jesus Christ as our personal Lord and Savior, these Christians who are now teaching this false doctrine are treading on extremely dangerous and serious grounds with God the Father.

This false heretical doctrine is going to lead a certain amount of people into hell because they will think they have all of the time in the world to accept God's free gift of eternal salvation through His Son Jesus, even to the point of believing they can accept this gift once they die and cross over to the other side.

To any of you who know other Christians who have fallen for this demonic doctrine, I ask that you continue to pray for them, asking God to bolt in there with His divine truth so they can get their wrong thinking straightened out on this very important issue.

We already have enough people who are going to end up in hell due to their own stupidity, stubbornness, and rebellion without making matters worse and teaching this kind of insanity, which is going to lead them even more astray from what the real truth is on how God has the big picture story of redemption all set up for the human race.

Jesus is Coming So People Get Ready!

About the Author

Bill Vincent is no stranger to understanding the power of God. Not only has he spent over twenty years as a Minister with a strong prophetic anointing, he is now also an Apostle and Author with Revival Waves of Glory Ministries in Litchfield, IL. Along with his wife, Tabitha, he, leads a team providing apostolic oversight in all aspects of ministry, including service, personal ministry and Godly character.

Bill offers a wide range of writings and teachings from deliverance, to experiencing presence of God and developing Apostolic cutting edge Church structure. Drawing on the power of the Holy Spirit through years of experience in Revival, Spiritual Sensitivity, and deliverance ministry, Bill now focuses mainly on pursuing the Presence of God and breaking the power of the devil off of people's lives.

His books 48 and counting has since helped many people to overcome the spirits and curses of Satan. For more information or to keep up with Bill's latest releases, please visit www.revivalwavesofgloryministries.com. To contact Bill, feel free to follow him on twitter @revivalwaves.

Recommended Books

By Bill Vincent

Overcoming Obstacles
Glory: Pursuing God's Presence
Defeating the Demonic Realm
Increasing Your Prophetic Gift
Increasing Your Anointing
Keys to Receiving Your Miracle
The Supernatural Realm
Waves of Revival
Increase of Revelation and Restoration
The Resurrection Power of God
Discerning Your Call of God
Apostolic Breakthrough
Glory: Increasing God's Presence
Love is Waiting – Don't Let Love Pass You By
The Healing Power of God
Glory: Expanding God's Presence
Receiving Personal Prophecy
Signs and Wonders
Signs and Wonders Revelations
Children Stories
The Rapture
The Secret Place of God's Power
Building a Prototype Church
Breakthrough of Spiritual Strongholds
Glory: Revival Presence of God
Overcoming the Power of Lust

Glory: Kingdom Presence of God
Transitioning Into a Prototype Church
The Stronghold of Jezebel
Healing After Divorce
A Closer Relationship With God
Cover Up and Save Yourself
Desperate for God's Presence
The War for Spiritual Battles
Spiritual Leadership
Global Warning
There Are Millions of Churches
Destroying the Jezebel Spirit
Awakening of Miracles
Deception and Consequences Revealed
Are You a Follower of Christ
Don't Let the Enemy Steal from You!
A Godly Shaking
The Unsearchable Riches of Christ
Heaven's Court System
Satan's Open Doors
Armed for Battle
The Wrestler
Spiritual Warfare: Complete Collection
Growing In the Prophetic
The Prototype Church: Complete Edition
Faith

To Order:

Email:
rwgcontact@yahoo.com

Web Site:
www.revivalwavesofgloryministries.com

Mail Order:

Revival Waves of Glory
PO Box 596
Litchfield, IL 62056

Shipping $5.00

If you mail an order and pay by check, make check out to Revival Waves of Glory.

Don't miss out!

Visit the website below and you can sign up to receive emails whenever Bill Vincent publishes a new book. There's no charge and no obligation.

https://books2read.com/r/B-A-XHBC-MHVQB

BOOKS 2 READ

Connecting independent readers to independent writers.

Also by Bill Vincent

Building a Prototype Church: Divine Strategies Released
Experience God's Love: By Revival Waves of Glory School of the Supernatural
Glory: Expanding God's Presence
Glory: Increasing God's Presence
Glory: Kingdom Presence of God
Glory: Pursuing God's Presence
Glory: Revival Presence of God
Rapture Revelations: Jesus Is Coming
The Prototype Church: Heaven's Strategies for Today's Church
The Secret Place of God's Power
Transitioning Into a Prototype Church: New Church Arising
Spiritual Warfare Made Simple
Aligning With God's Promises
A Closer Relationship With God
Armed for Battle: Spiritual Warfare Battle Commands
Breakthrough of Spiritual Strongholds
Desperate for God's Presence: Understanding Supernatural Atmospheres
Destroying the Jezebel Spirit: How to Overcome the Spirit Before It Destroys You!
Discerning Your Call of God

Glory: Expanding God's Presence: Discover How to Manifest God's Glory

Glory: Kingdom Presence Of God: Secrets to Becoming Ambassadors of Christ

Satan's Open Doors: Access Denied

Spiritual Warfare: The Complete Collection

The War for Spiritual Battles: Identify Satan's Strategies

Understanding Heaven's Court System: Explosive Life Changing Secrets

A Godly Shaking: Don't Create Waves

Faith: A Connection of God's Power

Global Warning: Prophetic Details Revealed

Overcoming Obstacles

Spiritual Leadership: Kingdom Foundation Principles

Glory: Revival Presence of God: Discover How to Release Revival Glory

Increasing Your Prophetic Gift: Developing a Pure Prophetic Flow

Millions of Churches: Why Is the World Going to Hell?

The Supernatural Realm: Discover Heaven's Secrets

The Unsearchable Riches of Christ: Chosen to be Sons of God

Deep Hunger: God Will Change Your Appetite Toward Him

Defeating the Demonic Realm

Glory: Increasing God's Presence: Discover New Waves of God's Glory

Growing In the Prophetic: Developing a Prophetic Voice

Healing After Divorce: Grace, Mercy and Remarriage

Love is Waiting

Awakening of Miracles: Personal Testimonies of God's Healing Power

Deception and Consequences Revealed: You Shall Know the Truth and the Truth Shall Set You Free
Overcoming the Power of Lust
Are You a Follower of Christ: Discover True Salvation
Cover Up and Save Yourself: Revealing Sexy is Not Sexy
Heaven's Court System: Bringing Justice for All
The Angry Fighter's Story: Harness the Fire Within
The Wrestler: The Pursuit of a Dream
Beginning the Courts of Heaven: Understanding the Basics
Breaking Curses: Legal Rights in the Courts of Heaven
Writing and Publishing a Book: Secrets of a Christian Author
How to Write a Book: Step by Step Guide
The Anointing: Fresh Oil of God's Presence
Spiritual Leadership: Kingdom Foundation Principles Second Edition
The Courts of Heaven: How to Present Your Case
The Jezebel Spirit: Tactics of Jezebel's Control
Heaven's Angels: The Nature and Ranking of Angels
Don't Know What to Do?: Discover Promotion in the Wilderness
Word of the Lord: Prophetic Word for 2020
The Coronavirus Prophecy
Increase Your Anointing: Discover the Supernatural
Apostolic Breakthrough: Birthing God's Purposes
The Healing Power of God: Releasing the Power of the Holy Spirit
The Secret Place of God's Power: Revelations of God's Word
The Rapture: Details of the Second Coming of Christ
Increase of Revelation and Restoration: Reveal, Recover & Restore

Restoration of the Soul: The Presence of God Changes Everything

Building a Prototype Church: The Church is in a Season of Profound of Change

Keys to Receiving Your Miracle: Miracles Happen Today

The Resurrection Power of God: Great Exploits of God

Transitioning to the Prototype Church: The Church is in a Season of Profound of Transition

Waves of Revival: Expect the Unexpected

The Stronghold of Jezebel: A True Story of a Man's Journey

Glory: Pursuing God's Presence: Revealing Secrets

Like a Mighty Rushing Wind

Steps to Revival

Supernatural Power

The Goodness of God

The Secret to Spiritual Strength

The Glorious Church's Birth: Understanding God's Plan For Our Lives

God's Presence Has a Profound Impact On Us

Spiritual Battles of the Mind: When All Hell Breaks Loose, Heaven Sends Help

A Godly Shaking Coming to the Church: Churches are Being Rerouted

Relationship with God in a New Way

The Spirit of God's Anointing: Using the Holy Spirit's Power in You

The Magnificent Church: God's Power Is Being Manifested

Miracles Are Awakened: Today is a Day of Miracles

Prepared to Fight: The Battle of Deliverance

The Journey of a Faithful: Adhering to the teachings of Jesus Christ

Ascension to the Top of Spiritual Mountains: Putting an End to Pain Cycles

After Divorce Recovery: When I Think of Grace, I Think of Mercy and Remarriage

A Greater Sense of God's Presence: Learn How to Make God's Glory Visible

Do Not Allow the Enemy to Steal: To a Crown of Righteousness, a Crown of Thorns

There Are Countless Churches: What is the Cause of Global Doom?

Creating a Model Church: The Church is Undergoing Considerable Upheaval

Developing Your Prophetic Ability: Creating a Flow of Pure Prophetic Intent

Christ's Limitless Riches Are Unsearchable: God Has Chosen Us to Be His Sons

Faith is a Link Between God's Might and Ours

Increasing the Presence of God: The Revival of the End-Times Is Approaching

Getting a Prophecy for Yourself: Unlocking Your Prophecies with Prophetic Keys

Getting Rid of the Jezebel Spirit: Before the Spirit Destroys You, Here's How to Overcome It!

Getting to Know Heaven's Court System: Secrets That Will Change Your Life

God's Resurrected Presence: Revival Glory is Being Released

God's Presence In His Kingdom: Secrets to Becoming Christ's Ambassadors

God's Healing Ability: The Holy Spirit's Power is Being Released

God's Power of Resurrection: God's Great Exploits

Heaven's Supreme Court: Providing Equal Justice for All

Increasing God's Presence in Our Lives: God's Glory Has Reached New Heights

Jezebel's Stronghold: This is the Story of an Actual Man's Journey

Making the Shift to the Model Church: The Church Is In the Midst of a Major Shift

Overcoming Lust's Influence: The Way to Victory

Pursuing God's Presence: Disclosing Information

The Plan to Take Over America: Restoring, We the People and the Power of God

Revelation and Restoration Are Increasing: The Process That Reveals, Recovers, and Restores

Burn In the Presence of the Lord

Revival Tidal Waves: Be Prepared for the Unexpected

Taking down the Demonic Realm: Curses and Revelations of Demonic Spirits

The Apocalypse: Details about Christ's Second Coming

The Hidden Resource of God's Power

The Open Doors of Satan: Access is Restricted

The Secrets to Getting Your Miracle

The Truth About Deception and Its Consequences

The Universal World: Discover the Mysteries of Heaven

Warning to the World: Details of Prophecies Have Been Revealed

Wonders and Significance: God's Glory in New Waves

Word of the Lord

Why Is There No Lasting Revival: It's Time For the Next Move of God

A Double New Beginning: A Prophetic Word, the Best Is Yet to Come

Your Most Productive Season Ever: The Anointing to Get Things Done
Break Free From Prison: No More Bondage for the Saints
Breaking Strongholds: Taking Steps to Freedom
Carrying the Glory of God: Igniting the End Time Revival
Breakthrough Over the Enemies Attack on Resources: An Angel Called Breakthrough
Days of Breakthrough: Your Time is Now
Empowered For the Unprecedented: Extraordinary Days Ahead
The Ultimate Guide to Self-Publishing: How to Write, Publish, and Promote Your Book for Free
The Art of Writing: A Comprehensive Guide to Crafting Your Masterpiece
The Non-Fiction Writer's Guide: Mastering Engaging Narratives
Spiritual Leadership (Large Print Edition): Kingdom Foundation Principles
Desperate for God's Presence (Large Print Edition): Understanding Supernatural Atmospheres
From Writer to Marketer: How to Successfully Promote Your Self-Published Book
Unleashing Your Inner Author: A Step-by-Step Guide to Crafting Your Own Bestseller
Becoming a YouTube Sensation: A Guide to Success
The Art of Content Creation: Tips and Tricks for YouTube
Signs and Wonders Revelations: Experience Heaven on Earth

Watch for more at
https://revivalwavesofgloryministries.com/.

About the Author

Bill Vincent is no stranger to understanding the power of God. Not only has he spent over twenty years as a Minister with a strong prophetic anointing, he is now also an Apostle and Author with Revival Waves of Glory Ministries in Litchfield, IL. Along with his wife, Tabitha, he, leads a team providing apostolic oversight in all aspects of ministry, including service, personal ministry and Godly character.

Bill offers a wide range of writings and teachings from deliverance, to experiencing presence of God and developing Apostolic cutting edge Church structure. Drawing on the power of the Holy Spirit through years of experience in Revival, Spiritual Sensitivity, and deliverance ministry, Bill now focuses mainly on pursuing the Presence of God and breaking the power of the devil off of people's lives.

His books 50 and counting has since helped many people to overcome the spirits and curses of Satan. For more information or to keep up with Bill's latest releases, please visit www.revivalwavesofgloryministries.com. To contact Bill, feel free to follow him on twitter @revivalwaves.

Read more at https://revivalwavesofgloryministries.com/.

About the Publisher

Accepting manuscripts in the most categories. We love to help people get their words available to the world.

Revival Waves of Glory focus is to provide more options to be published. We do traditional paperbacks, hardcovers, audio books and ebooks all over the world. A traditional royalty-based publisher that offers self-publishing options, Revival Waves provides a very author friendly and transparent publishing process, with President Bill Vincent involved in the full process of your book. Send us your manuscript and we will contact you as soon as possible.

Contact: Bill Vincent at rwgpublishing@yahoo.com

Printed in the USA
CPSIA information can be obtained
at www.ICGtesting.com
LVHW041350020823
753718LV00003B/531